Learning a Language

How I managed it.
How you can, too.

IAN GIBBS

Learning a Language
©2018, Guid Publications
Bruc, 107, 5-2
08009 Barcelona
Spain
Email: guid@guid-publications.com

Cover design: Andy Meaden
Interior design: Estudio Hache

ISBN:
978-84-948660-0-5 paperback
978-84-948660-1-2 ebook

This book is dedicated to my wife, Olga,

for her patience, understanding and proofreading.

Content

Introduction

"The conquest of learning is achieved through the knowledge of languages."

–Roger Bacon, 13th century philosopher

In October 2016, I was having a coffee with Gillian, my publisher, who pointed out that as I'd just finished my first book, I clearly had more free time on my hands than was good for me so why not start a second one.

"Well, I've been putting together this idea for a story." I said, "It's based on Cinderella but with the heroine as an anorexic sociopath and her step family as all really nice people!"

Apparently oblivious to this outstandingly promising idea, Gillian explained what she had in mind involved following up *The Sorites Principle* with looking at how to apply its theory to practical situations such as getting fit or raising perfect children.

"I'm not exactly the best person to talk to about getting fit or raising perfect children." I said, sulkily pouting over my café con leche.

"There is one you do know about. Learning a language. You taught yourself Spanish from scratch and you're surrounded by language learners, aren't you? Using the Sorites Principle, how quickly could someone learn another language?"

"I don't know" was my concise answer.

"Good. Then why don't you find out?"

And so it was that 2017 saw the start of a new chapter in my life: how to learn a new language by applying lots of little actions continuously over six months to see how far it would get me.

Despite what my publisher might think of me, I'm certainly not an expert on language learning. She was right about teaching myself fluent Spanish. But to be honest, I've no recollection of how I actually did it. So a little research was in order.

I spent two months trawling through webpage after webpage, reading up on how the experts recommend learning a new language. I watched the videos, downloaded the apps and slowly started to formulate my own plans.

Although I didn't know much about language learning, I did know quite a bit about how we think, how we behave and how the two are connected. It was interesting to see why some of the things recommended by the experts would work and why some of them wouldn't—at least not for me.

Contrary to these multilingual gurus, I'm not overly enthusiastic about learning new languages. I'm not the sort of person who wakes up and decides to learn Aramaic before breakfast. Learning a new language is a major challenge and not one I particularly get excited about. But to be honest, I think that's a strength because most people who want to learn a new language aren't that enthusiastic about it either. They want to learn it not out of some deep-rooted burning desire but out of necessity. They need it to get a job or a qualification or because they're going to need it to survive.

So I amassed loads of theory and filtered it, formulating my own list of what would most likely work for someone with only a mild interest in the subject.

But once I had settled on my list, I realised if I wanted anyone to take me seriously I was going to have to put my theory into practise. I was going to have to learn a new language myself.

This presented me with a problem. What language should I learn?

The traditional languages studied by the British are French, German and Spanish. I'd already taught myself Spanish, I did a bit of French at school and all I knew about German was it's a language where "A young lady has no sex, but a turnip does", which didn't appeal much. Then there where the bigger ones such as Chinese, Russian and Arabic which sounded exotic but with which I had no foreseeable connections.

These are important points to bear in mind. As I point out later, if you're going to invest your time and effort into studying a language, you really need a good reason to do so—and as far as reasons go, 'having to learn ANY language just to prove a point' wasn't going to be enough.

Then I realised I had the answer right under my nose. I live in Barcelona which is the capital of the autonomous Spanish community of Catalonia.

Catalonia has, in addition to Spanish, its own language: Catalan (about 85% of Catalonia's population speak it). It's a 'Romance' language, which has nothing to do with candlelit dinners and everything to do with the Romans. Apart from the educated few (who wrote in Classical Latin), most Romans spoke Colloquial (or Vulgar) Latin. When these people decided to retire and move abroad in search of the good life, they took their language with them which over the centuries evolved further to become what it is today. This is how Catalan, Italian, French, Spanish, Portuguese and Romanian came to be. In short, Catalan is a sort of halfway between Spanish and French.

If you speak Spanish, you can get along perfectly well in Barcelona without speaking a word of Catalan. My mother-in-law (originally from the Spanish province of Burgos where they definitely don't speak any Catalan) has lived in Barcelona for fifty years and still struggles to string a single sentence together in the local language.

Catalonia is dominated by Spanish in many ways. Most of the music is in Spanish, as are most of the books, films and television stations. But there is one sector where Catalan wins hands down: education. By local law, all state-funded schools must have Catalan as their main language. So most kids grow up in Catalonia speaking Catalan, including mine.

Before I became a father, Catalan was something that happened to other people elsewhere. But as I now have two seven-year-olds, I find Catalan has slowly crept into my family life. Parent-teacher meetings are held in Catalan and most of the conversations you hear at school are in Catalan. In fact, I'm told Catalan is the most successful minority language in Europe with the other minority languages such as Gaelic, Irish and Welsh looking on enviously at how well the Catalans have established a language that was once banned and moribund.

So I decided to learn Catalan. By doing so, I'd be able to understand the parent-teacher meetings without needing the wife to translate. I'd be able to understand my kids, though their English and Spanish is fine. I'd be able to talk with the other Catalan-speaking parents of my children's classmates. Furthermore, there's a lot of kudos associated with the language. Since Spanish is almost always the default language to learn for foreigners coming to Barcelona, if you learn Catalan, the locals get really impressed and that was absolutely fine by me.

So this book is not about the theory of language learning. It's about how to do it in real-life the way I managed to do it myself. After six months I was able to converse in the language and felt quite proud about it. But I'm not going to try to persuade anyone it was easy.

One of the problems with learning a language (with learning anything, in fact) is it's one of those things that, along with learning to tango and hiking around the world, happens step by step, little by little and as such requires that dreaded word: perseverance.

There's lots of ways to start learning a language—via books, multimedia or human beings—but there is just one reason most of us stop. And that is by giving up before we've achieved our objective. This can be done consciously by actively making the decision to give up, or unconsciously, which is what happens when you look at the calendar, do a bit of mental calculation and get all surprised when you realise it's been over two months since you last conjugated a verb.

I worked as an English teacher in my first few years in Barcelona and once had a surprisingly man-to-man talk with the language school director who let me into a 'little secret' of his which was this: the problem with running a language school wasn't getting students to sign up to start new courses. It was getting them to keep studying all the way to the end of the academic year.

It was shortly after this that he hit upon the somewhat radical idea of 'adjusting' the contract so that, unbeknownst to them, new students were actually signing a loan agreement. This meant, in reality, that they were paying for their entire course upfront and then paying off the loan month by month afterwards. So when their perseverance ran out after the first term and they stopped attending, they were surprised, then confused and finally indignant to discover they still had to continue paying back a loan for a course they no longer wanted. The school went bust shortly afterwards as students flocked to the competition.

Some would say it's our teacher's fault if we lose interest and want to drop out. I partly agree, but even the best teachers lose adult students during the academic year. It's fairer to put the responsibility squarely on our own shoulders. If we've decided to embark on a new endeavour which we know is going to be long and arduous and then give up before completion, it is nobody's fault but our own.

We can easily come up with excuses (it's too boring, too difficult, too time-consuming...) but at the end of the day we have the choice to do something about these excuses. But we don't. We give up. After all, quitting is so easy, isn't it? And persevering is so difficult—or at least it used to be.

Here is where this book comes in: how to learn a language by applying The Sorites Principle which states that the constant application of insignificant actions, when coherently focussed, will inevitably lead to dramatically significant results. Or, in other words, it's about how to learn a language by carrying out lots of little actions that are so easy, persevering with them is child's play compared to dragging yourself once a week to an evening class.

Or in even simpler words, it's about how to learn a new language and keep going until you succeed.

I hope you find it useful.

One final observation before we begin. I don't think I'm sexist. By this I mean I'm not one of those people who is hung-up about women. I don't hold with sexual stereotyping. I certainly don't think men should be the breadwinners or women make bad bosses. But looking through the pages of this book, there is undoubtedly far more references to men than women. The reason for this is very simple: Almost all of the top well-known polyglots and linguists I've come across are men. I'm sure there are just as many women who've learnt multiple languages, but their presence in the publishing charts or on Ted Talks is very weak indeed. They just don't seem to want to get on the world stage and talk about it. I'm very sorry if there are any great female authors/polyglots who I have overlooked. Honestly, I did try.

"As the direct result of learning Hindi, I've had some of the greatest career, cultural, social, and spiritual experiences of my life. I've made dear friends I could never have met or communicated with, and I've learned things that would have been much harder to learn without the language skills. Is learning a language a good use of your time? Absolutely."

—Chad Fowler, American writer, programmer and public speaker

In a Nutshell

"The constant application of insignificant actions when coherently focussed will inevitably lead to dramatically significant results."

– The Sorites Principle

Many of the big, important changes we want to make, like learning a language, happen gradually. As the time it takes is long and the changes are small, we become frustrated. We confuse slow progress with no progress. We consider our little actions to be insignificant and our pessimistic attitude creates a self-fulfilling prophecy: We give up, we fail.

This is a problem.

The solution to this problem can be divided into three steps: Planning Your Goal, The Pieces of the Puzzle and Perseverance.

Step 1: Plan Your Goal

Identify exactly what you want to achieve.

When are you going to start? When do you want to have it finished? Is the definition of your objective easy to understand? Is your goal easily measured? How are you going to know when you've reached it?

Expressions like 'getting fit', 'being more successful' and 'learning a language' are all examples of goals that are annoyingly imprecise and subjective. They can mean different things to different people. What for one person is 'learning a language' is 'messing about with a phrasebook' for another.

Define your goal in terms of specific numbers, dates, places, values and durations.

'To be able to have a simple conversation in Italian' is not a good goal. It's too vague.

'To have a 2-minute conversation in Italian with an Italian waiter in Rome next August' is much better.

Try to answer as many of the questions regarding what, where, when, who, why, how long, how much and how many (the question of 'how' by itself we'll be looking at in a moment).

Once you've clarified your goal, you can pass on to the next step.

Step 2: Pieces of the Puzzle

Close your eyes and imagine yourself having successfully learnt the language of your choice.[1]

Now, continue to imagine all the things you'll have done to get there: all the work, all the actions carried out, the materials acquired, the websites visited, the enrolments and matriculations, all the books read, all the exercises done, all the conversations practised. They all combine to form one great picture of success.

1- I know you can't read the text with your eyes closed, but you get the idea, don't you?

Now, just like a big jigsaw puzzle, imagine this picture to be broken up into thousands of tiny pieces, with each piece representing just one of the little actions you had carried out.

All you need to do, to get from where you are now to where you want to be, is to carry out each one of those actions. Take each piece of the puzzle and put it into place.

"Okay," you might say, "so each piece represents one hour of studying and after six hundred hours I'll be able to speak my target language, right?"

Not quite.

There is much more to learning a language than just studying. In fact, as we'll be seeing in the next section, studying is overrated. There are many other actions, (such as downloading a dictionary, listening to podcasts or talking to yourself in the shower). So many, I've dedicated a whole section to them (see chapter 3).

This is the answer to the 'How?' question from the previous page:

Q: How are you going to learn your new language?

A: By carrying out lots and lots of little actions every single day.

Just like little drops of water can eventually fill a bucket, lots of little actions can steadily accumulate, building up into a satisfyingly impressive achievement.

Once you've identified all the little pieces of your puzzle, all that's left is to put a few of them into place every day until you finish.

Doing something every day until you get to the end requires perseverance. That's why it's the third step.

Step 3: Perseverance

For some, 'Perseverance' might as well be a four-letter word.

It can provoke a wince, a grimace, a 'shall-we-talk-about-something-else' sort of reaction.

If this is you, please bear with me just for a moment longer.

If perseverance conjures up images of stress, tedium or some sad bloke pushing a giant stone ball up the side of a hill, then think again. It doesn't have to be like that at all.

You've been getting up in the morning for how many years now? Is that Perseverance?

You've watched a total how many hours of TV so far? Is that Perseverance?

How many cups of tea drunk, or miles walked, or biscuits eaten?

Perseverance is defined as 'persistence in doing something despite difficulty or delay in achieving success'. But what if our 'something' was so simple you couldn't consider it difficult, and what if, instead of one big far-away goal, you had lots of little sub-goals?

When we break down our goal into lots of little pieces, the difficultly tends to disappear. Each piece is simple and easy rather than difficult and daunting.

Listening to a bit of Russian radio while you make your breakfast is easy. Looking at one page of an Italian comic is easy. Spending two minutes revising Malayan vocab while you're on the loo is easy. Just like cleaning your teeth, they are simple things that don't require a willpower made of titanium. And the more, the merrier.

Instead of focussing on your big end goal, if you define a series of small sub-goals such as 'by the end of tomorrow I will have carried out eight of my little actions', then you don't have to wait for what seems like eternity to reach your objective. You can get that feeling of 'mission accomplished' within twenty-four hours.

Breaking your big goal into small actions is just one technique to improve your persevering power. There are many more and we'll be looking at all of them in the following pages.

If you learn how to apply them all, you'll be able to learn languages you hitherto only dreamt of. You'll surprise your family and amaze your friends. You'll become a master in the art of language learning.

But first, let's consider the nature of the beast we're dealing with. The Laws of Physics govern how our physical world works, The Laws of Nature govern our flora and fauna. It only seems reasonable that in order to understand how language learning works we need to familiar ourselves with The Laws of Language Learning.

The Laws of Language Learning

"The simplicities of natural laws arise through the complexities of the language we use for their expression."

– Eugene Wigner, Hungarian-American mathematician

Learning to Drive

When a person starts learning to drive, they already know a few of the universal laws about driving, such as:

1. It's a good idea to be over a certain age.

2. It's a bad idea to drive while incapacitated by drugs or alcohol.

3. It's a good idea to drive on the same side of the road as everyone else going in your direction.

4. Refuelling or recharging every now and then is a good idea, too.

And there are many others. Some of these laws might seem obvious. Nevertheless, it's still important to recognise they exist.

Though not as commonly known, there are also universal laws concerning language learning. Some of them are also more obvious than others. But if you're going to start learning a new language, it's definitely a good idea to know them.

During my research, I realised that every expert has their own opinion on the laws of language learning. Some of them almost everyone agrees with, while some of them are more unique. After having tried out every piece of advice I could get hold of, I sifted through them to refine, combine or decline them as I've found best.

I don't claim they're perfect. I'm sure you might like to make a few changes of your own. My objective is to make you more aware of the language learning process and to maybe think about it in a different way. So please feel free to adjust where necessary.

Law 1: You Can Do It

Some activities are easier to do if you are physically built in a certain way.

It's easier to play basketball if you are tall. It's easier to read tiny writing if you have good eyesight. Let's face it, if you don't have the necessary physical appendage some activities can be almost impossible. Similarly, some 'soft skill' activities are done better if you are highly creative or have a good emotional intelligence.

You might be tempted to say, 'I don't have what it takes to learn a new language'.

But the fact that you expressed this statement in a perfectly well-structured sentence using the correct grammar, vocabulary and pronunciation demonstrates, contrary to your opinion, you definitely do have what it takes to learn a language.

Learning to speak a language has nothing to do with emotional intelligence or I.Q. I know some fantastically stupid people who are capable of speaking most eloquently.[2] I admit, the language in question is their mother tongue but at one point, they couldn't even speak that. But they were able to learn it without any problem, just like you and I did. If you did it once, you can do it again.

There are millions of people on this planet who never studied languages at school. But despite this, they are still able to speak several. In Nigeria, there are over 500 languages actively spoken. It's not at all unusual to be able to speak three or four languages there. About a quarter of the population of Switzerland speaks three languages or more, too. Even in the city where I live, Barcelona, most people are bilingual, if not trilingual. In fact, in many parts of the world, only being able to speak one language is considered unusual. But these people are not gifted. They have the same mental capacity as you and me.

If they can do it, you can do it, too.[3]

Law 2: Adults Learn Languages Better Than Children

Common sense tells us only young children can learn languages well. After all, look at how well you learnt to speak English before you were six and look how pathetic your French was after 'years' of French classes at school.

But I suggest you pay less attention to 'common sense' and more attention to the real evidence.

The only reason why young children learn their mother tongue is they have no other option. If they want to express themselves, ask for something, get help or just fit in with the rest of their peers, they have to do it in their mother tongue. What's more, their learning process is continuous. It's full immersion 24/7. It never stops. But (and it's a big 'but') even though

---

2- I bet you do, too.

3- I left school with the worst grade in Spanish it was possible to get. I hated my Spanish classes. I was rubbish at it. What was the point anyway? I was never going to need to speak Spanish, I was never going to live in Spain and I certainly wasn't going to have any Spanish family. I now live in Barcelona. I've been here for twenty-seven years. My wife is Spanish. My children are half Spanish. I work, rest and play in Spanish—a language that I can now speak perfectly fluently. It just goes to prove you never know about these things.

the average six-year old has spent 72 months in intensive practice, their language level is still dishearteningly basic.

If you were to go to some exotic tropical island where no one spoke English, after six years of working, socialising and interacting with the locals in the manner of your choice, your ability to communicate in their language would far exceed the capability of a native six-year-old to express themselves.

Adults learn better than children. This is because we have already acquired so many mental skills, thought processes and accumulated knowledge to learn new stuff. Our linguistic foundations are much stronger than that of a child.

Let's look at an example, shall we?

If I say to you that, from now on, the letters 'zj' together are pronounced exactly the same as 'sh' in English, how would you pronounce the following words?

cazj, zjugar, fizjing, zjampoo, Englizj, ozjean, muzjroom

As an adult, you should be able to pronounce all of them without too much effort.

I tried to teach my kids how the letters 't' and 'h' together are pronounced 'th'.[4] We worked on it for weeks, yet they still struggled. But as adults we have a vast vat of knowledge that we can dip into for help for learning new stuff. You have decades of experiences, knowledge and ideas that can help you absorb and assimilate. As an adult, you have a much greater capacity for learning a new language than young children do.[5]

4- I'm well aware that 'th' has a voiced AND unvoiced pronunciation, as in 'this' and 'thistle', but I haven't gone into that yet, so please don't write in.

5- The one exception to this is pronunciation. There is clear evidence that young children learn to distinguish small differences in pronunciation and are able to finely adapt their pronunciation to perfection. Our ability to do this diminishes from six years. This is why adult Spaniards struggle to tell the difference between ship and sheep. The linguistic difference, although 'obvious' to native Anglophones, is very small and very challenging to the Spanish who have no equivalent phonemes in their language. But apart from that, we adults win hands down.

Law 3: Practice Is More Important Than Theory

I passed my driving test in 1982.

Those were the good old days of learning to drive. You found someone with a car who'd accept ready money for putting their personal safety at risk. You'd get in, fasten your safety belt and off you'd go. Nervous, jittery and extremely wobbly around corners, but that was what learning to drive was in those days.

Nowadays it's different. We have this 'theory' thing which as far as I'm concerned has taken all the adventure out of the learning-to-drive business. You have to sit in a classroom for months before you even get a chance to sit in the driving seat.

I bring this up because learning to drive and learning to speak a foreign language are very similar. They both involve theory and they both involve practice.

It's important to point this out. One key reason so many of us fail at learning a new language is we spend far too much time on the theory and nowhere near enough time practising. We pass hours and hours with our noses stuck into our 'teach yourself' manuals. We study vocabulary and grammar. We learn to conjugate irregular verbs ad nauseam. Then one day we decide to go for our first linguistic drive. We find a real person to talk to. We think of all the options for what we are going to say. We open our mouth and... stall. Ouch! We get it wrong. We get lost for words. Our pronunciation goes pear-shaped. We feel embarrassed and incompetent, and our natural response is to withdraw. The result is a total linguistic breakdown. We deduce our problem is due to a lack of study and return to our books.

This is a mistake.

Our inability to hold the simplest of conversations in a new language isn't due to a lack of theory. It's due to a lack of practice. If, when we stalled our car for the first time, we'd said 'Oh, bother, I need to go back and study my urban velocity limits', your instructor would think you were a bit mental. Jittery driving is what you have to go through before you can become a capable driver. So it is with speaking a new language. You have to accept that having embarrassingly pathetic conversations doesn't mean you're failing. It means you're succeeding in passing through that painful period where your brain can't work as fast as your mouth would like it to.

I'm pointing this out because most of us want to learn a new language in order to communicate, and the best way to learn to communicate is to practise doing just that—communicate: to have real conversations with real people. If you're of a gregarious disposition, you won't have a problem with this. There are extroverts amongst us who happily launch themselves into staggered conversation with anyone they can find. I've seen them happily waving their arms about and laughing at their own linguistic inadequacies. But I'm not like that, and in all likelihood, neither are you. You probably feel rather uncomfortable about talking to an unfamiliar person in an unfamiliar language. Your tendency is to shy away from it until you've studied a bit more—studied enough for that strange and unfamiliar language to feel not so strange and unfamiliar any more.

I'm sorry to break the bad news, but it's never going to happen. The single most productive thing you can do to learn a new language is to start communicating—from day one, if you dare. That is how we really learn a language—through social interaction, not by studying from books. It's how kids learn. It's how the experts learn. And if you want to make some serious progress, then it's how you are going to learn, too.

Seven years after I left school with no ability to converse in Spanish whatsoever, I moved to Barcelona. I never attended Spanish classes. I never did an online course. Nevertheless, for the first few years, I shared a flat with three girls—Núria, Cristina and Maria—none of whom spoke much English. I had no other option than to start practising from day one.

So start getting used to the idea you're going to be conversing in your chosen language with other people sooner than you thought. It's not going to be easy. It's not going to be comfortable. But if you go about it the right way, it'll be fun, exhilarating and a damn sight more productive than just keeping to the theory.

Law 4: You Don't Have to Live in a Country to Learn its Language

I'll be introducing you later on to some of the heroes of language learning: people who have learned to speak multiple languages. Some of them have achieved this by travelling abroad but others haven't.

Travelling is no longer a prerequisite for successful study, and these contemporary examples prove it. Neither does living in your target language country guarantee you being able to speak it. I know I've just explained how I learnt Spanish by living in Barcelona but the city is bilingual (Spanish and Catalan). After living here for twenty-six years, my ability to converse in Catalan was almost zero. I never paid any attention to Catalan and I certainly never tried to speak it. I know several Anglophones who've been here in Barcelona for more than a decade but their level of Spanish and Catalan is pitiful. Why? Because they make hardly any effort to improve. They spend very little time focussing on the language and practising it.

Conversely, it's also perfectly possible (especially in this shrinking cyber-connected world) to focus on your target language and practise it even if you live thousands of miles away from the nearest native speaker. You can do this in so many ways. It's easier than ever to read it, listen to it, speak it and partake in real conversations with real native speakers—all without leaving the comfort of your own sofa. Language has nothing to do with your geographical whereabouts and everything to do with how much you focus on learning it.

Law 5: Make Pronunciation a Priority

There is something highly emotional about pronunciation. If we native Anglo-Saxons speak English while putting on almost any foreign accent, the result is usually hilarious.[6] I think it's curious we have such a strong emotional response to hearing a French, Chinese or German accent. Seeing French, Chinese or German written down just doesn't provoke the same response. It's the distinctive pronunciation that counts.

6- Try it for yourself, spend the day talking to everyone in the foreign accent of your choice and see what happens. Go on—I dare you.

When you start learning a language, especially from the comfort of your own home, you'll probably feel silly putting on a funny foreign accent. You'll feel uncomfortable about making your mouth move in new and mysterious ways which would only produce mirth and ridicule if your friends could hear you.

The sad result is we resist putting on the accent. We play down its importance. We learn to massacre a language at the same time as we learn to speak it.

It's not just that we regard putting on an accent as uncomfortable or silly. There are other factors involved, too.

Much of our study is inevitably from written material; consequently there is little guidance to pronounce the words correctly. Getting access to the right pronunciation can be difficult. I've listened to computer-generated pronunciations with dismay. There is still so much progress to be made with them.

In contrast to the mental effort to learning a new language, learning the new pronunciation is physical. It requires moving our mouth in ways that are not natural. Our mouths don't like doing things that are not natural. Our brain sympathises with our mouth and says 'That'll do' well before we have achieved anything close to what would be considered acceptable by a native speaker.

In fact, our brains seem to have a pronunciation filter. When we hear a new word pronounced in a foreign language, our brain breaks it up into bits of sound, approximating each one to the nearest corresponding sound (or phonemes) from our own language. When we try to replicate this new word, we use our own familiar phonemes to say it. The result is an approximation to the new word. But, like a teapot made out of Lego, the result is not as effective as you might have hoped for.

Because of this, you tentatively start a conversation in your target language, only to be faced with a perplexed native who has no idea what you've just said. Your native gabbles out something in response, but as you aren't familiar with the correct pronunciation, you're completely lost and confused. This is a frustrating experience for both of you and one which is unlikely to make you feel good about yourself or your target language.

When I started to learn Catalan six months ago, I already understood the importance of pronunciation. So I made an effort to get pronunciation right. After just a few weeks, the strangeness started to wear off and now speaking Catalan with the right pronunciation feels completely natural.

So let's get this straight. From the very beginning, you really have to make a big effort to get to grips with the new pronunciation. It's part of the deal. You can't have one without the other. Don't just learn to speak French, learn to speak French in a proper French accent.

Yes, it will feel strange, uncomfortable or even silly to start with. But get a grip. This is what language learning is all about.[7]

Law 6: Forget the Grammar (for the Moment)

If pronunciation is one of the most underestimated key parts to language learning, grammar is one of the most overestimated.

Although grammar is an intrinsic part of any language, it's simply not necessary to understand it in order to have a decent conversation. I don't understand how the internet works, but I can still look for videos of cute puppies. I don't claim to understand women, but I've managed to keep my marriage off the rocks for twelve years so far.

Understanding grammar is not a key requirement for conversation. As Khatzumoto[8] says "Learning grammar in order to use a language is like learning organic chemistry in order to make a sandwich." After all, do you understand English grammar? If the contraction of 'Are you not?' is 'Aren't you?', why isn't the contraction of 'Am I not?' 'amn't I?'?

You don't need the grammar; you just need to learn the language.

7- For a few tips on improving your pronunciation, see Appendix C.

8- Khatzumoto is author of AJATT, the website http://www.alljapaneseallthetime.com. If your new target language is Japanese, this website is a must.

Consider the basic expressions:

Hello!

How are you?

My name's Sam.

I'm studying Greek.

I've been studying for five months.

The first is an interjection. The second a present simple question form. The third involves a possessive pronoun and a contraction. The fourth is present simple continuous and the last is present perfect continuous involving a verb that can be can be either transitive or intransitive. Do you need to know any of that to have the conversation?

Of course not.

At no point do we sit our kids down, wrench the iPad from their tiny hands and explain how to use the subjunctive or what gerunds are all about. It just isn't that important when you're starting out. I agree it's useful to know a bit of grammar at the right time. Knowing the rules can help consolidate your knowledge. But if you really want to learn your target language as quickly and effectively as possible, put your grammar book in the bottom drawer, out of harm's way, and invest your time more wisely practising your useful phrases, vocabulary and pronunciation.

Law 7: Learn the Gender of Everything—It's Important

Whoever it was who invented languages where the whole universe is divided up into things that are considered either male or female has got a lot to answer for. As a simplistically-minded English speaker, I just don't get why a glass should be considered 'male' and a cup 'female'. I mean, really, what is the point? All it does is confuse. How can they not see that it all works perfectly well without any gender being arbitrarily assigned to anything?

Ranting aside, we have no alternative to accept this divisive yin-yang obsession of carving the universe up into two groups (or even more, given that some languages have a neuter gender, too). It's not natural for us Anglophones but there's no option other than to get on and learn it.

It's important not only for communicating fluently but also because some words can totally change their meaning depending on their gender. In Catalan, for example *'un clau'* (masculine) is a nail—something you hammer into wood—whereas *'una clau'* (feminine) is a key—something you open a door with.

Often, there are general rules of thumb that work well. In French, the majority of nouns that end in '- e' or '- ion' are feminine (with the exception of words ending in '- age', '- ege', '- é', or '- isme'. In Italian, many nouns ending in '- i' or '- o' are masculine and nearly all nouns ending in '- e' or '- a' are feminine. But there are always exceptions.

So how does one go about learning the arbitrary gender of hundreds (and eventually thousands) of inanimate objects and abstract concepts?

The best way I've found so far is to go back to the yin-yang and use it in your favour. Yin-yang is the Chinese philosophical way of considering the universe to be made up of opposing yet complimentary forces.

Clearly invented by a man, 'yin' is considered **feminine**, passive, negative, inwards, downwards, cold, liquid and so on, whereas **'yang'** is masculine, active, positive, outwards, upwards, hot, aerial, et cetera.[9]

But this can come in very useful when learning language genders and here's why.

Suppose you've just learned a new word in Spanish. Let's say it's 'mano', the word for 'hand', which for some reason in spite if it ending with an 'o' has been deemed feminine. So as feminine Yin is also cold and wet, then imagine your hand also being cold and wet—very cold and very wet. Imagine your hand has just spent ten minutes in the freezing-cold Arctic ocean. It's painfully cold. It's turned blue and now has small icicles starting to form from your fingertips. Imagine the feeling. Imagine the pain. Remember this image every time you think of the word 'hand' in your new language. The striking image of a blue-veined, hypothermic, shivering hand will stay with you forever and with it, the ability to remember that hands are female regardless of how large and hairy they may be.

9- With the Romance languages, the concept of 'reason' is considered female and 'mistake' is male. This suggests to me the genders were more likely assigned by a woman.

Similarly, you can do this with masculine things. In Spanish, the word for 'shoe' is 'zapato' which even if it has a six-inch stiletto, is still considered masculine. Masculine is yang. So now imagine the shoe to be hot, very hot. It's glowing red. It's on fire! With every step you take you leave scorched footprints. As you walk you can smell the acrid vapours of burned carpet! Again, this image, along with the gender, will stay with you for life.

The key to this is to **make the associated image as sensually extreme as possible.** We are genetically programmed to remember sensual data. If something is painful, it's best to remember it so we can avoid it in the future. If something is nice, we want to remember it so we can go back and get more when nobody's watching.

But what about the neuter gender, you might be asking if you're studying German or Polish. Well, following the yin-yang idea, where yin and yang exist in equal amounts, you have peace, harmony and balance. So if you come across a new word that is considered neuter, such as the word for 'baby' (which in German, conveniently is 'Baby'), imagine the baby to be quiet, asleep, snuggly warm, happily lying in its cot glowing in peace and harmony. It's neither too hot nor too cold. It's not dripping through the mattress or exploding in your face. It's very existence is tranquillity. If you can keep this image with you, you can remember its linguistic gender is neuter.

Law 8: Wait to Conjugate

Another linguistic concept most foreign languages haven't fully grasped yet is just how needlessly complicated conjugation is. I keep pointing out to anyone who I can get to listen that this is all you need:

I can

You can

He/she/it can

We can

They can

and that's it. Even the third person singular 's' is redundant. But until we reach the age of enlightenment, we're stuck with a target language with a whole range of frustratingly illogical and irregular conjugations.

Just because there's a gorse bush at the bottom of your garden doesn't mean you have to get up every morning and throw yourself in it. Just because your target language has lots of nasty conjugations for each of its confusing tenses it doesn't mean you have to spend a demoralising amount of time trying to remember them all.

I know a ten-year-old called Cadence who tried to learn Spanish. Her family regularly holidayed on the Spanish Mediterranean coast and she was fascinated by this new and exciting language. Her school didn't teach Spanish, so Cadence started to teach herself. She was making great progress. She was learning lots of new words and expressions. Her parents were impressed with her new skill and, when on holiday, would send her off to run errands such as going to ask for the bill in a restaurant. All went well until she discovered verb tenses and conjugations. Hundreds of them: Present Indicative, Present Perfect, Preterit, Future Continuous, Imperfect Subjunctive, Imperative… Each verb having dozens of confusing forms. She tried to learn the basic conjugations for the most common verbs, but it was all too irregular, confusing and frustrating. It just didn't work. What started off as something fun and interesting started to become difficult and demotivating. Her enthusiasm for Spanish subsided and she lost interest.

Please understand this: **You don't have to learn how to fully conjugate any verb in all its forms to be able to communicate.** It's a phenomenal waste of time and effort when you're starting a language to learn all the verb forms. Stick to the ones you need. Trying to remember all of them is unnatural and pointless. Be aware of their existence by all means. Get an idea of how they are formed. But just focus on learning verbs in the form which are most useful to you. Get the most out of your studying time by learning the phrases and expressions which you are likely to need or which interest you most.[10] As you continue to build up your vocab, the different verb structures and forms will slowly start to click together. You'll start to get a 'feel' for how different verbs change according to their circumstances. You'll start to learn conjugations and tenses the way the native speakers do —through experience.

But at some point after you've studied for many months, you'll have acquired sufficient language to genuinely want to strengthen your verb

---

10- See next section on chunking.

structures. If you feel it's the right time, if you feel genuinely motivated to do so, then great. Be my guest. But there are ways of learning the conjugation of verbs that work better than others.

I still remember from my schooldays French classes *'Je suis, tu es, il est, elle est, nous sommes, vous êtes, ils sont'* but even though we learnt it by rote, I have never, ever had a conversation that went *"Bonjour, mademoiselle. Je suis, tu es, il est, elle est, nous sommes, vous êtes, ils sont, peut-être?"*

All you achieve by rote-learning the conjugation of verbs is how to reproduce by rote the conjugation of verbs. Trust me on this one: It's not the most useful of conversational ice-breakers.

When you feel it's the right time to learn verb conjugation, it's much more productive to learn the different conjugations in context—to use the form of the verb in a way you are much more likely to encounter in the real world. You can achieve this by explaining how different family members or friends do the same verb. It's a sort of 'conjugation explanation.' The way it works for me is to have an imaginary conversation with a friend about your corresponding families.

If we were practising the verb 'to receive', the conversation would go something like this:

I receive ten emails a day.

You receive twenty emails a day.

So between us *we receive* about thirty emails each day.

Your brother receives twenty emails a day, too.

So you and your brother receive forty emails.

Your sister receives fifty emails, so *your brother and sister receive* ninety emails together.

Not the most riveting of conversations but I find it much more useful than the usual 'I receive, you receive, he / she / it receives, etcetera.' It's a good way to practise conjugating unfamiliar verbs. It also allows you to practise important little words such as 'about', 'so' and 'too'.

The reason why this sort of conjugation explanation works better than the 'I-am-you-are-she-is' variety is it gives you both a context and a structure. When you carry out this method of conjugation, it might seem longwinded but instead of mere repetition (a thought process seldom used in real conversation), your brain is having to deal with the language in a much more realistic way. Even though your context is imaginary, it's still a context. As you repeat the sentences to yourself, you can visualise the people you're referring to and you can imagine the circumstances you're referring to.

This means when you find yourself in a similar situation in real life, retrieving that particular language point will be much easier. You won't have to go through your 'I-am-you-are' stuff until you get to the right conjugation form. It's not learning purely by repetition.; it's learning by giving contextual meaning to the language.

Law 9: Don't Learn Words Individually, Learn Them in Chunks

Language, to a certain extent, is highly predictable. When we talk, we do so referring to a specific subject or theme. If my particular theme is that I'm feeling thirsty, then the words I use will be centred around drink and the possibility of acquiring it. I'm unlikely to start using words like century, candle and fluffy. These words have nothing to do with the subject of quenching my thirst.

Words tend to herd; they travel around in groups.

Consider 'milk', for example. 'Milk' is commonly found in the company of nouns such as 'glass', 'bottle' and 'carton', verbs such as 'drink', 'pour' and 'spill' and adjectives like 'fresh', 'cold' and 'semi-skimmed'. In fact, it's difficult to have a meaningful conversation without using its common associates. They go together. Consider the following:

A pint of beer

A cup of tea

A liquid lunch

Milk and sugar

A gin and tonic with ice and a slice.

These combinations are so common they are worth learning together as an expression or 'chunk'. In language learning, 'chunking' is about learning words that frequently appear together and it's a very efficient way of learning.[11]

Take the verb 'to love', for example. As a normal transitive verb, 'love' can be preceded by any direct pronoun such as 'he', 'we' or 'they' and followed by any of the indirect pronouns such as 'him', 'us', 'them'. This means we have dozens of grammatically correct combinations such as 'You love them', 'It loves him' and 'They love us'. But even though these are correct, the number of times we come across them is nothing compared to the combination of 'I love you'.

If you're just starting, it's much more efficient to learn the expression 'I love you' rather than learning the verb 'love' by itself and then trying to figure out how to put it into a sentence later on.

So when you find a new word you want to learn, don't just learn it by itself. Put it together with a few of its commons associates. This way, when it comes to having a conversation, you'll be able to retrieve the appropriate chunk and use it automatically.

Let's say you've just found the word for 'pen'. You might be tempted to write out a revision card[12] with the word pen, but another option is to write out two or three example sentences or chunks that might be useful. These might be:

Have you got a pen?

This pen doesn't work.

The pen is mightier than the sword.

But how can you tell which words commonly go together? Although 'salt and vinegar' go together in English, in Spanish they just think it's strange.[13]

11- *'Ich bin eine Berliner'*, *'Viva España'* and *'Voulez-vous coucher avec moi ce soir?'* are good examples but unlikely to be useful all at the same time.

12- We'll be looking at revision cards in much greater detail later on.

13- This is absolutely true. In Barcelona, vinegar is just for the salad. If you're in a restaurant and ask the waiter for some vinegar to put on your chips, everyone in the restaurant stops eating and stares as if you've just committed blasphemy (such as, for instance, saying Barcelona Football Club is rubbish).

The context of where you came across the word should give you a clue. Pay attention to where you found your new word and what other words were accompanying it.

If the context of where you came across the new word doesn't offer any clues, you could start off by considering some of its basic properties. If it's a noun, does it have a gender? Is it a countable noun? (Your dictionary will answer these questions.) Even the simplest of chunks such as 'a pen' or 'the pen' are better than just learning the word for 'pen' by itself.

If it's a new verb, you can have a good guess at what might commonly go with it. You don't have to be Einstein to come up with chunks like 'read a book' or 'learn a language.' But be careful, it's not that simple. Consider these comfortable and not-so-comfortable chunks:

'Have you cleaned your teeth?' and 'Have you washed your teeth?'

'Do you want to watch the telly?' and 'Do you want to see the telly?'

'Make your mind up' and 'Do your mind up'

'I speak five languages' and 'I talk five languages'

In each example, one of these is 'right' and the other is 'wrong'. But when you start to think about it, the only real reason why this is so is because 'It's the way we usually say it'.

To check out your educated guesses, you can do a search for "common expressions using 'pen'", ask someone who knows or post the question on your forum group.

Whether it's an adjective-noun set (a nice hot cup of tea) or a common expression (I'll do it tomorrow), these chunks of language are easy to learn.[14] You don't need to understand the syntax or grammar; you just need to remember the chunk. Each chunk is a little piece of the puzzle that represents your target language. As you learn more and more chunks, you'll naturally formulate your own rules about what feels right and what feels wrong. This is exactly how we learnt our mother tongue. You've done it once and you can certainly do it again.

14- Do you know why we say, 'a nice hot cup of tea' but not 'a hot nice cup of tea'? Me neither.

Law 10: Learn Functional Language First

If you were to go and sit quietly at a bar where your target language is spoken, I bet you'd hear lots of language that has hardly anything to do with grammar at all. Much of our everyday language are short phrases or even just single words that convey very specific sentiments or attitudes in a very succinct way. Linguistically, these are known as interjections. All of the following are interjections:

Hey!

Wotcha!

Cheers,

Bless you,

Bother,

Brilliant,

Thanks.

Wow!

Oh my god!

Ouch!

No!

Please!

Sugar![15]

Alright?

Yes.

Okay.

Good night.

Good luck.

Goodbye!

With a bit of imagination, these words could almost represent an entire conversation by themselves. They are a basic part of general conversation and as such are precisely the sort of stuff you need to start learning straight away.

15- Or whatever it is you usually say when, at the very last minute, you remember it's the wife's birthday and that it's now far too late to do anything about it.

They are tiny chunks in their own right. We've already considered the importance of chunking, but this law states there is chunking and then there is useful chunking. Learning how to say your aunt's pen is on the table or your hovercraft is full of eels is all very nice examples of chunking in theory but it's all very useless in practice. There are dozens of predictably common situations where we need to talk to other people, such as asking for permission or help, to explain or clarify, to apologise or to give information (see appendix E for common functional language). These involve equally common structures that behave in very predictable ways. You are far better off learning these chunks of conversation. They will serve you well in times of need.

Of course, your times of need might be very different from those of the next person. If you are the private owner of a small import/export company that transports raw fish products via marine services, the expression 'My hovercraft is full of eels' could be a useful expression to learn. It's your choice. But whatever you choose to learn, focus on functional language first and skip the rest until later.

Law 11: Embrace Embarrassment

One of the key messages in this book is the importance of practising your new language by speaking it as much as you possibly can. No matter what level you are, the best way to continuous improvement is to get used to using the unfamiliar language you've just learnt.

This is a major challenge.

Trying to communicate in a new, unfamiliar language to new, unfamiliar people is extremely difficult. It's embarrassing, let's face it.

In fact, if you're anything like me, even in English, talking to anyone unfamiliar is a challenge. I'm not exactly an extrovert. To be honest, I struggle with banal chitchat. I find it difficult to strike up the simplest of conversations at parties. I much prefer to sit quietly with a glass of something relaxing and observe. So, having a challenging conversation in a challenging language can appear to be an insurmountable problem.

The only way to deal with this problem is to bite the bullet and do it. The most effective way to approach a complete stranger and start a conversation is by approaching them and starting one.

But when you're feeling shy and have the vocabulary of a Janet & John book, it all seems so much easier said than done. But it's just like jumping off the top diving board: It looks much worse than it really is. Once you've done it and survived, doing it a second time isn't so difficult.

One thing you can do to help yourself to get past the shyness is to: 1) smile; 2) make sure you are able to reproduce most of the top 30 useful phases for beginner conversation (see Appendix D); and 3) remember it's an important step towards reaching your goal. At worst, you're not going to understand each other and the conversation will end. At best, you will be able to communicate, you'll get some much-needed experience, you'll help store important phrases into your long-term memory and you might make a friend. I'd say the risk is worth it.

You can also help reduce your xenoglossophobia[16] by explaining to a study buddy, positivity donor or friend how important it is to get real conversation practice. Ask them for support in helping you take that first step to initiating a conversation in your target language. (More about these important people later.)

Another thing you can do to deal with shyness and embarrassment is to talk to people who are in a similar situation as yourself but coming from the other direction: people who are learning your language. There are more ways than ever to meet people who speak the language you're studying and who are studying the language you speak, including clubs, forums, language exchanges and apps.

By doing so, you are immediately striking up conversation with someone you already have something in common with—learning a language. I'm not saying you're going to get on with them like a burning barn, but at least your mutual levels of empathy and patience will be higher than if you're trying to talk to someone you just met in a bar.

16- Xenoglossophobia: the feeling of worry, nervousness and apprehension experienced when trying to use a new language and sounding like a wally.

When you first start conversing with the outside world, it requires a substantial mental effort from you just to recall and pronounce the limited vocabulary you've memorised so far. The time delay required in order to carry out this herculean effort, along with the inevitable facial expressions and arm-waving, might make you think you're giving the impression of someone with a reduced capacity for rational behaviour, or to use the vernacular, that you sound like a wally.

Like it or not, this is an intrinsic step to language learning. Before you can start to sound smooth, suave and sophisticated in your target language, you have to start by sounding like someone who is trying to get to grips with a new language. Don't worry about it. All language learners go through this stage. Even Queen Elizabeth I, who is purported to have been able to fluently speak ten languages, had to start off by sounding like a wally, too. So although you won't be giving the impression of someone who is verbally in command of their speech, you will be giving the impression of someone who has the balls to make the effort to learn a new language. And that, in the ears of a native speaker of your target language, counts for a lot. So get used to the idea, relax and enjoy the ride.

Without doubt, the best way to deal with any fear, whether it's starting a conversation in your target language, making a parachute jump or speaking in front of an audience of five hundred, is to just do it. Don't think about it too much. The more you deliberate, the less likely it's going to happen. The guiding rule is if you doubt for more than three seconds then you've missed your chance.

It's like going down the big slide for the first time, or jumping off the top diving board. Once you've done it, you'll realise it wasn't so bad. You survived! And maybe, just maybe, the thrill of making that achievement might spur you on to have another go.

Law 12: Make Mistakes

Another reason why we are embarrassed to open our mouths when learning a language is the fear of making mistakes.

You need to accept this now: You are going to make lots of mistakes and it really isn't a problem. My kids are well on their way to becoming trilingual in English, Spanish and Catalan. Do they speak any of these languages perfectly? No. Do they make mistakes? Yes, all the time. Are they bothered about it? Not in the slightest. Are their levels of language improving? Absolutely, every day.

Making mistakes—or to be more exact, not getting it absolutely perfect—is all part of the learning process. Expect to make mistakes. Look at them in a more positive light. Making mistakes shows you are stretching yourself, stepping out of your comfort zone. This is a good thing. In some ways, the more mistakes you make the better, because not only does it show you're really pushing yourself, but it also helps desensitise you to slipping up occasionally. And when I say 'occasionally', I mean in the course of one day you can be proud of yourself if your mistakes run into triple digits. That's right: It's perfectly alright to be making hundreds of mistakes every day.

We're not taking an exam, we're learning how to communicate in a new language. You do this by trying stuff out, by playing around with the language, by exploring, probing, seeing what works and what doesn't. It's trial and error. The more mistakes you make, the more it shows you're trying. In fact, you can make as many mistakes as you like, so long as you follow the next rule.

Law 13: Learn from Your Mistakes

You're walking along a forest path when you come to a pleasant little glade. There, sunning itself on a tree stump, is an adorably cute, fluffy little animal that looks like a cross between a kitten and teddy bear. As you approach, it closes its little round eyes and rolls over on its back, apparently inviting you to tickle its tummy. You kneel down by its side and reach out to touch its warm and fluffy underbelly. In a flash, the little animal jumps up and savages your arm off at the elbow.

Ho hum… You won't be making that mistake again, will you?

We're very good at not making the same mistake twice when we need to. But many are the language exchanges I've had where the other person has made an important mistake and, upon correction, simply carries on without making any note about it only to then, a few moments later, do exactly the same thing again… and again and again.

Sometimes we're so engaged in our conversation we don't want to pause to make notes. We believe having been corrected means we'll get it right next time. Sometimes, we don't even consider the mistake important enough to make it worth learning. I've had language exchanges with people who don't even bring anything to write with to the session. This for me is like going shopping without a shopping bag. You might be able to walk away with a couple of items at best, but you would do so much better if you were properly prepared to carry all your newly acquired goodies, wouldn't you?

Some mistakes are more important than others. It's for you to decide if a mistake is worth trying to learn. But I'm tempted to say all the mistakes you make are important. If it was something you actually wanted to use in order to communicate then, yes, I'd say it's worth learning properly.

If you know, without doubt, you will never need to use that bit of language ever again, then no, leave it. It's not worth the effort. But if it's something you've stumbled over more than once, then it's very likely worth learning. So make a brief note of it, then take time later to set it down nicely, check you've got it right, incorporate it into your revision cards and make an effort to use it correctly next time. That is what learning is all about.

Law 14: The Obstacle Is the Way (or Mind the Gap)

As you go along developing your new language, reading, speaking or writing, you're going to encounter gaps in your vocabulary—new words and expressions you'd like to say but don't know yet. Some of these are going to be words that have little use for you; obscure words that are only useful in very rare or specific situations like 'ball-bearing', 'jugular' or 'logarithmic'. On the other hand, there will be words you discover you need which are much more useful. Words which you're likely to come up against frequently. These are the words you should be learning.

This sounds so obvious. But it's often ignored.

What usually happens when you don't know the thing you want to say is you look it up or ask for help. But then the temptation is to carry on without making any note about the new word. It's tempting to think it's no big deal—it's not worth bothering about. After all, you didn't make a mistake; you just had a bit of a gap.

These gaps are important. They are signs saying 'Here's a useful expression. You needed it just now and you'll probably need it again'. I completely recognise it's impossible to learn every single new word you come across. If you're just starting with a new language, your brain would melt and dribble out your ears.

But it's important to take a second and jot each one down. By the end of the conversation, you'll have a small collection of new words. That is the time to go through your list and select the ones you think are going to be most useful. Those are the ones to concentrate on, to put into your revision system (Law 16).

Law 15: Write Stuff Down

When the productivity guru David Allen was asked what, in this great technology era, a person needed to be super-productive, his answer was "get something called a 'pen' and get something called a 'piece of paper'… and write stuff down." His point being that our brains are built to have ideas, not to remember them.

We are fantastically bad at remembering stuff. It takes great effort to recall the simplest of things. We try to remember something but we get interrupted, we get distracted, we get given other stuff that needs remembering, too. The result is you find yourself standing in the kitchen unable to remember what you came there for.

By the way, let's not confuse 'remember' with 'learn.' You are capable of learning millions and millions of things. You are able to hold a really impressive amount of stuff in your long-term memory. But that's not the same as remembering. Remembering is putting stuff into your short-term memory. In exactly the opposite way to your long-term memory, your short-term memory can't do much better than hold the number of things you can count on the fingers of one hand before it starts struggling.

If you start with the idea that you're not going to be able to remember anything at all, you won't be far off the mark.

We've already seen how writing down the stuff you get wrong and the stuff you don't know how to say yet is a sound idea. But writing down the things you want to learn extends much further. When you are reading, take time to write down any interesting bits of new language you discover. When you're watching something on YouTube or listening to a podcast, write down anything of interest worth remembering. Don't expect to still have it in your head by the end of the programme. You won't. You probably won't even remember you were supposed to have remembered it. Something else will have already caught your attention.

Write down stuff when you revise. **Write down what you think is the right answer BEFORE you check**. It is so easy for us to convince ourselves the answer we came up with is the answer on the back of the card. The only way to prove yourself right is to write it down first and check it afterwards.[17]

Writing down the vocab and expressions that you want to learn is the best way of clearly identifying it, trapping it and studying it until you're sure you can release it into your long-term memory without fear of it disappearing into thin air.

Law 16: Revise as Often as You Can

Learning is all about putting information into our long-term memory.

Occasionally this happens in a flash: You get stung by a wasp and instantly you learn it's better to steer clear of them. You try a gourmet rum truffle and instantly learn you could spend the rest of your life eating them. Some experiences are visceral; they immediately stick.

17- It's also a good way to check spellings and accentuation, too.

Unfortunately, new language rarely has the same effect on us. I don't know of anyone who has listened to a speech or watched a theatre production for the first time and were so impressed they found they could repeat the whole thing word perfect.

Revision is really important. As Samuel Johnson said, "People need to be reminded more often than they need to be instructed." The way we learn new language is by active repetition; by using it again and again and again as often as possible. By as often as possible, I mean not just once an evening but several times throughout the day, every day. Each revision doesn't have to be long—a minute or two is enough, whenever you can squeeze it in.

As we will be seeing later on, the best way to revise is not by going through old texts and rereading stuff. Effective revision means revision cards. As we'll be discussing, these can now be real ones you can keep in your pocket or digital ones you can keep in your smartphone. Whichever you choose (and you can choose both if you like), they are going to be one of your most frequently used language learning tools.

Law 17: There Is a Hierarchy to the Activities of Learning

Not all language learning activities have the same impact on your language acquisition. There's a hierarchy to language-studying activities, with some being more effective than others:

Reading about your target language in your mother tongue is acceptable but…
…it's not as good as *reading in your target language*.

Reading in your target language is alright but…
…it's not as good as reading while listening to a recording or watching it on video.

Passively watching or listening to a recording is fine but…
…it's not as good as actively trying to remember the language and repeat it out loud.

Repeating your target language out loud is good but...
...it's not as good as improvising a conversation with yourself.

Improvising a conversation with yourself is great but...
...it's not as good as practising conversation with your teacher/language exchange partner.

Having a conversation with your teacher/language exchange partner is fantastic but...
...it's not as good as having a real conversation with a real person in a real-life situation.

Having a real conversation with a real person in a real-life situation is the best way of learning your target language.

You should be looking at how you are going to be able to make this happen.[18] The other activities are all perfectly valid. There's a place for all of them in your language learning programme. But it's easy to focus on the lower-level ones. They are more within our comfort zone.

The most effective way of learning is to be doing more higher-level activities. Consider the different activities you are carrying out to learn your target language. How far up the hierarchy are you going?

Law 18: Make it Fulfilling

If you read enough articles about language learning, you'll soon come across one that says language learning should be enjoyable. I think it's really important to clarify this idea because it can be so easily misleading.

If you are averse to learning your target language, if you find learning your target language to be boring, a grind or a waste of time, if you loathe and detest your target language with every fibre in your body, then you are going to find it very difficult to make real progress. Your subconscious mind will simply reject it.

18- In other words, how can you start having general conversations with native speakers? Don't worry if you can't think of the answer. In this cyber-connected world, it's becoming easier every day to talk to people all over the planet for free. It's really quite exciting when you think about it. We'll be looking at this later, too.

If you're going to learn a new language as effectively as possible, you need to have your mind as open to it as possible. The best way to do this is to make it fulfilling.

Consider marathon runners. On the face of it, a marathon runner has to be some sort of masochist. Think about what you have to go through to be one. Training for hours in all weather conditions, running until your whole body aches, until your torso and legs are in agony, until you feel your heart is going to explode. It can hardly be said to be 'fun.' It's not fun. It's bloody difficult and painful. But in spite of this, millions of people worldwide run marathons. Why?

It's because they find it fulfilling.[19] Marathons are social activities where you can put yourself through hell and back in the company of your marathon colleagues who are all doing exactly the same. It's to do with comradeship. It's to do with proving to yourself you can do it. It's to do with getting fit. It's to do with bragging about it in the pub afterwards and comparing times and positions.

It's not so much about 'fun' as 'fulfilment'.

People run marathons, climb mountains and travel to the frozen poles not because it's a laugh but because it satisfies a part of their soul. It meets some inner need that yearns to be met.

If you are totally ambivalent towards your new language, you're not going to progress very much. But if you can find some need within you, some want, some desire, something you need to achieve, acquire or prove, your chances of persevering with your goal and making rapid progress towards it are improved tenfold.

Language learning doesn't have to be fun,[20] but it does have to be fulfilling. We'll be looking how to do this in chapters 6 to 13.

19- I have to confess I'm not one of them. Given the choice between having to run a marathon or being waterboarded, it's a tricky dilemma which would require careful calculations of pros and cons. Though I expect the waterboarding would finally come out on top so long as it doesn't last too long.

20- Of course, if you can make it fun *and* fulfilling, all the better.

Law 19: Be Prepared to Lose Yourself

If someone were to describe your personality, they might use words like witty, charming, extrovert, frank or diplomatic. All of these characteristics are reflected by the way you talk, the words you use and the way you pronounce them. Our accent is a mark of where we're from and the tribe we belong to. The unique way we express ourselves through our language is called our idiolect. Whether it's a turn of phrase, a favourite adjective or a creative way of pronouncing a word, our idiolect is what makes us who we are.

Most of us like the way we express ourselves, that's why we do it. We consciously or unconsciously decide what to say. Rarely is the way we speak something we do against our will. In our mother tongue, we are confident and comfortable. Our first language is like a pair of well-worn jeans—a practical fashion statement which gives and stretches exactly where it's supposed to.

But your new language isn't like that. Your new language is more like a brand new cheap pair of ill-fitting jeans that have been badly made out of something akin to cardboard. Your new language doesn't allow you the flexibility and freedom you're old familiar one does. When you're starting out, it's difficult to be charming or witty or diplomatic when all your language level can afford you are monosyllabic grunts.

If you're not prepared for the full impact of this new linguistic handicap, it can come as a shock. If you're used to being a bit of a chatterbox or a know-it-all or a sympathy-aunt, it's a daunting experience to discover you're now the strong silent type.

As you steadily build up your new language, you will find new ways to get it to stretch and bend to your sociolinguistic needs. Slowly you will find your favourite turns of phrase and start to develop your own idiolect and through that, your own personality. Little by little, your new target language will stop feeling strange and start becoming a comfortable outfit you can easily put on whenever you want.

But at first it will feel strange to be unable to come across as the-person-who-you-are. Strange but perfectly natural. As a new learner, you're about to go down into a long dark tunnel. But don't worry. It's not endless. Your 'new you' is patiently waiting for you where that little light is at the end.

Law 20: Learn Something Every Day

The last, but by no means the least, law of language learning (learning anything in fact) is to do something every day until you've nailed it. There is an immense power to mentally (or physically) stretching yourself regularly every day over a long period of time. It is one of the most undervalued and underutilised abilities we have. Little by little we really can move mountains.

And yet we don't.

It's easy to start out promising ourselves we'll study regularly but it's not at all so easy to stick to it.

There is a little voice inside us that says it won't hurt to skip today and make up for it by doing twice as much study tomorrow.

This is a huge mistake.

In this case, you are putting off doing something today and delegating it to your future-self. When you do this, you are naively hoping your future-self will be prepared to do something your present self isn't.

The reason why your present-self doesn't want to do whatever-it-is today is most likely due to lethargy, stress, distraction or bad memory (Oh my God! Is that the time? Oh, well, I'll do it tomorrow). Of course, by doing this you are assuming your future-self will not be as tired, stressed, distracted or forgetful as you are at the moment.

Who are you trying to kid? Your future-self will be feeling exactly the same as you are at the moment, if not more so.

So do your future-self a favour and stop delegating. Do your homework today. Do it now. The more you get accustomed to doing a little bit of study today, the easier it'll be to do another little bit of study tomorrow.

The inverse is also true.

If you accept, just for today, you're going to skip your study (or your diet, your writing or your workout), the more likely you'll do exactly the same thing tomorrow. This goes on and on until one day you look at the calendar and realise it's been weeks since you last did something constructive. It's a trap so easy to fall into. I know. I'm speaking from first-hand experience.

One January, I joined the local gym with the most earnest of intentions to go swimming there three times a week, which I was assured would do wonders for my bad back. I managed to do for the first month or so. But then I started to slack, going just once a week, or once a fortnight, until October came and I realised I hadn't been to the gym since before the summer holidays. So much for good intentions.

So get used to the idea of learning a bit of language every day.

Even better is to get used to the idea of a little bit every morning, every lunchtime, every evening and every night. Nothing too challenging, just a little something every few hours. But anything is better than nothing. This is the key to the Sorites Principle, the key to making it all happen.

If you follow these Laws of Language Learning every day for even just a few weeks, you'll start to notice the difference.

Exactly how to do this is what the rest of this book is about.

Questions

- Which of these language learning laws are the most important for you?

- Could you adapt any of them to fit your needs better?

- Are there any you think are missing?

- What would you have to change in your language learning sessions to follow these rules?

Case study 1: Brenda[21]

I first met Brenda while I was giving a presentation in Marbella. She has an unstoppable sense of humour and more than her fair share of 'laughter-lines'. She is what you might consider a modern day 'Shirley Valentine'. She took early retirement, told her husband to go stuff himself, sold up and moved to Costa del Sol where she joined a group of friends living the Life of Riley on the Mediterranean Coast.

That was in 2010. For the first few years, she tried to learn Spanish with little success. One of her problems was that she was living in a cocoon of Englishness. All her friends were English speakers, she watched the English TV channels, got the English newspapers and even the local restaurant was owned and run by English speakers. Another of her problems was that she was regularly visited by General Futility. In spite of annually enrolling in Spanish classes at the local Community Centre, where her teacher 'tried hard but was dull and boring', she was uninspired and didn't feel she was making any real progress. She got frustrated by 'constantly' having to go over the same things in class (I'm sure her teacher felt the same). She had come to believe she was incapable of learning another language and it was all a complete waste of time.

Of course, one of her main handicaps was that she spent most of her time speaking, hearing, reading and writing in English. Her Spanish studies were sporadic and half-hearted. Predictably, her perseverance was less than satisfactory. One of Brenda's mistakes was that she was relying on her own opinion to gauge whether she was making any progress or not. Nevertheless, Brenda felt very bad about not speaking the language of her new place of residence and she was determined to set things right.

So Brenda embarked upon a coherent plan of action which included the following.

- She needed to make Spanish interesting and fun. She also needed peer pressure. So she started her own group of three friends which soon became seven. 'The Magnificent Seven' they called themselves, quite appropriate for a bunch of retired women. From the very start they

21- I used Brenda's Case Study at the end of *The Sorites Principle*. I've included it here again because it's exactly the sort of thing this book is about.

were all similarly frustrated by their lack of Spanish and were keen to make some 'real' progress. They would meet twice a week: Once in a 'Not English' restaurant (which was a different venue each time) for a study-lunch and once in the home of one of the members where they would watch a Spanish film on DVD with Spanish subtitles.

- When they met in the restaurant they would insist the menu be in Spanish and that the waiter would talk to them in Spanish. They took it in turns to translate the menu. Anything on the menu that they didn't understand would be noted and learnt for the following week.

- They made an effort to get to know the local Spanish population by having a guest speaker come to their meeting who would talk about their interests. It turned out the mother of the girl from the post office was the winner of the prestigious local Spanish Omelette competition and they got her to come round and give them a cookery class one day.

- Once word got around about the Magnificent Seven, they started to get invited to various places. They got taken round a local vineyard and were shown how wine was made. They got shown round a local paper manufacturer and learned how paper was made. One old neighbour came round and tried to teach them how to play the guitar. They even got this woman to come round to give them a presentation about sex toys which she said was absolutely hysterical and even though they didn't buy anything they did learn a lot of new vocabulary!

- Instead of a study-book, each person in the group would carry a little notebook— their version of a Goal Diary—where new vocabulary and useful expressions were noted down and shared at the meetings.

- Brenda bought a set of multi-coloured Post-its which she used to label things around the house and for useful phrases of the week.

- They also started to discover Spanish music. They would listen to songs and try to understand the lyrics. Sometimes one of them photocopied the lyrics and then tippexed out some of the words as a sort of gap-fill exercise. As they started to discover Spanish music, Brenda would listen to it for pleasure instead of her usual listening selection from the 60s and 70s.

- There was real peer pressure to improve. Everyone made an effort to come up with ideas, activities or games. One of them brought in Trivial Pursuit in Spanish, but as Brenda admitted, "We were all rubbish at it. But it was a laugh anyhow." Anything that was new and seemed useful was presented and noted down. Anyone who didn't contribute at the 'useful words I've learnt this week' part of the meeting was 'severely chastised'.

- They actively helped each other. If someone knew something that the others didn't then they would teach it to them. It made everyone feel useful. There was real learning and progress taking place.

- Rather than estimating her own progress, she started to count how many hours 'studying' she had completed each day on the understanding that any mental application to speaking Spanish was positive.

- They got hold of past exam papers for the Spanish as a foreign language diploma or DELE (*Diploma de Español como Lengua Extranjera*), the first A1 level and practised the parts they didn't know.

All seven of them sat their first official Spanish language exam and all seven of them passed with flying colours. As Brenda said, "It was like being a kid again. It was so exciting. When I saw my result it was like YES! I've done it. I've done it! We were all just a bunch of giggly girls."

Questions

- If you've tried to learn a language before, does any part of Brenda's story sound familiar?

- Is there anything Brenda did that you might like to have a go at?

- Is there anything she did that you'd do differently?

- Does Brenda's story give you any ideas of how you could improve your language learning strategy?

- What else could you learn from Brenda's experience?

Your Goal

"If the goal you've set for yourself has a 100 percent chance of success, then frankly you aren't aiming high enough."

– Benny Lewis, Polyglot founder of *Fluent in 3 Months*

What Exactly is your Goal?

It might seem like a redundant question at this stage after having acquired a book on language learning.

But seriously, what exactly is your goal? Do you really want to learn a language? Which one? What level do you want to get to? What do you want to be able to do in your target language? When are you going to start? How many months are you going to study for? When is your finishing date?

Being able to speak a language is not a straight 'yes' or 'no' process. It's not an all or nothing deal. This might sound obvious but it's not something I understood as a teenager.

Do you remember Spielberg's 1977 film *Close Encounters of the Third Kind*? There's a scene, about two thirds in, where the French-speaking UFO investigator Claude Lacombe is in one of those military portacabins, having a polite argument with the American base commander Major Walsh with the help of an interpreter.[22] In this scene, Lacombe is asking questions to the Major in French which are then translated by the interpreter into English. But then, halfway through, Lacombe stops talking in French and says (in a heavy French accent) "Eet eez steell a meestery why zey are 'ere. Even zey do not know why - Leesten to me, Major Walsh, eet eez an event soseeolojical." And at this point I thought 'That's stupid! If the French bloke can speak English, then why is he wasting everyone's time using an interpreter? Why doesn't he make life easier for everyone and just speak English?"

What I was too naïve to appreciate in 1977 is that speaking a language is not an all-or-nothing concept. It is a sliding scale. You gradually go from nothing to fully proficient in small stages. You might be alright saying somethings (such as 'Listen to me') but be a bit dodgy on others (such as 'marshmallow'). So if you are interested in learning a language, then it's useful to have a clear idea of what level you want to reach and what your immediate objectives are. If you want to become fluent in a new language, you have to go through all the intermediate stages first. You have to learn to walk before you learn to run, as they say.

As we'll be looking at in the section on Patience, it's important to focus your attention not on your long-term goal but on your short-term goals. This means identifying the sort of things you need to learn first, sticking to them and not trying to be a smartarse by trying to learn too much, too soon.

To give you an idea of what the different language levels are, the Common European Framework of Reference for Languages (CEFRL) was set up to try to categorise how well someone knows a language by putting them in six levels: Beginner, Elementary, Intermediate, Upper Intermediate, Advanced and Proficient (for more details see appendix A).

22- For those of you interested, Claude Lacombe was played by the French film director François Truffaut, Major Walsh was played by Warren J. Kemmerling and the interpreter was Bob Balaban.

One rule of thumb is a language course studied in a Language Centre from September to June for three hours a week (about a hundred hours in one academic year) is expected to take you up one level.

However, if you're more serious about improving your language level, it's perfectly reasonable to double this speed and go up two levels in one year. If you really are super-keen, you could even manage three or four levels depending on the time you can put in, the effectiveness of your learning method and the difficulty of your target language (See appendix B for language difficulty ratings).

My Goals

For my own efforts at language learning, when I started on the 7th January 2017, I set myself two goals:

- To pass my Intermediate Catalan Certificate exam on the 3rd June 2017; and

- To give a 10-minute public presentation in my new language 4th July 2017 at the Catalan Toastmasters Club, 'Som-hi'.

Each of these objectives was clear, specific and measurable.

The first of these meant passing my exam within five months (7th Jan to 3rd June). My initial level was what's called False Beginner. I knew Spanish which has much in common with Catalan. But despite this I was still unable to hold even a simple conversation in the language. So I was really starting out at the beginning of Elemental. Sitting my Intermediate exam meant covering two levels in just two terms. This turned into just four and a half months when I discovered my exam had been brought forward to the 20th of May. Ouch!

My second goal, which turned out to be much more challenging, was to give a public ten-minute presentation in Catalan to a live audience of about fifteen people on how I had taught myself Catalan in just five months. I'm a member of the international public speaking organisation Toastmasters and there is one group in Barcelona, 'Som-hi', that hold their meetings in

Catalan. Of my own freewill, I volunteered to go to their club and give a speech explaining the techniques I had used to learn the language and what I had discovered in the process.

Both of these goals served me very well to keep me on track. Without these clear and specific objectives, my learning would have been much more arbitrary—without direction or as much motivation.

Considering I was unable to string together any sort of coherent conversation when I started, the challenge was definitely on.

Measurables

How can you tell if you're making real progress?

You must have a way of accurately measuring your progress if you want to do things properly. Taking exams is one way of measuring. But exams happen once or twice a year which is not what you need. You need to see yourself progressing on a much more regular basis if you're going to use your progress to motivate yourself.

Another way is to go by someone's opinion about how well you speak. But I don't recommend this. Opinions are not reliable, whether your own or from others. When you're feeling demotivated, your self-assessment will be far too critical. Equally biased will be any friend's opinion of your achievements so far. What's 'You're doing great' supposed to mean exactly? If you were 'doing great' last week as well, does that mean you've learnt exactly the same amount of stuff? And what if you don't agree? Who's right? And how can you tell?

No, opinions are not satisfactory.

The most concrete measurable I've identified so far is to count revision cards. You can count them and therefore measure them. Not how many revision cards you've made but the number of cards you can remember correctly.

If each card has a chunk of new language with an average of, say, two to three new words and you make four revision cards a day, that corresponds to learning approximately ten new words a day or about 300 words in a month.

Once a week, take time to go through all your revision cards. Some will be so easy you can skip them (but be honest about this, you're only cheating yourself if not). Go through the rest and add the total up. You can then compare the result to last week's for irrefutable proof of your progress. This is important as we'll see later in section 7.

Why

One way to estimate how well you are going to succeed in persevering with any project is to consider how badly you want it to become a reality. Learning a language is no exception.

If you 'quite fancy' the idea of speaking Japanese because it's a cool thing to do at parties but otherwise have absolutely no other interest in it whatsoever, then I'm afraid your chances of drumming up what it takes to get to fluency level are zero.

If, however, you find yourself (for some bizarre reason which we shan't go into) trapped, penniless and starving to death in some isolated Japanese village, then the likelihood of you soon learning the local lingo is 100%. You have all the motivation you need.

Your reasons for learning a language can come in many shapes and sizes. Furthermore, they are constantly changing, they increase in intensity or they suddenly disappear altogether.

When I first came out to Barcelona, my motivation to learn Spanish was nothing more than a mild interest since I didn't intend to stick around for more than a couple of years and most of my newly found friends were fellow Anglophones. But when I met an interesting and highly attractive Spanish girl who for some inexplicable reason seemed to have similar opinions about myself, my reason for wanting to improve my Spanish increased, in a very literal sense, overnight.

Our reasons for wanting to achieve something can change—due to naturally occurring external forces (like suddenly finding you have a romantic interest) or by your own conscious thought process (like deciding you're tired of being regarded as a linguistic failure and want to prove them wrong once and for all).

It is important to be aware of your motives for learning your target language. This is because at some point in the future, you are going to need each and every one.

In a nutshell: If you are serious about wanting to learn a language, the more reasons you can amass to persuade yourself to do so, the better.

So what are the possible reasons for learning a language and how many of them can you apply to yourself? Here are a few to consider.

1. To increase your employment prospects
2. To improve your mental health
3. To date exotic people
4. To make yourself stand out
5. To make friends
6. To give yourself added value
7. To impress
8. Because it's your destiny
9. To learn a secret code
10. To irritate
11. To get attention
12. To face the fear and do it anyway
13. To save money
14. To travel more
15. Because the universe wants you to
16. To improve your travel experience
17. To learn about a new culture
18. To enjoy a new culture
19. Because it's fun
20. To have more sex

21. To develop self-confidence

22. To live overseas

23. To become more open minded

24. To fit in

25. To stretch yourself mentally

26. Because it's interesting

27. To grow your network

28. To make more money

29. Because it makes you feel superior

30. To fight off boredom

31. To make yourself more useful

32. To be accepted

33. To keep up with the Jones

34. To cut out the middle man

35. To be happier

36. To be more competitive

37. To insult people without them knowing

38. To be the best you can be

39. To keep yourself mentally active

40. To communicate with extended family

41. To gain independence

42. To prove to yourself you can still do it

43. Because it's a form of self-expression

44. To help people

45. To do something different

46. To realise a dream

47. To influence others

48. To win a bet

49. To prove a point

50. To write a book about it

Some readers might find shocking the idea someone would want to learn a language for capitalistic, psychological or carnal gains. But the world doesn't rotate on culture and world peace alone. We all have our own world views. We all have our own agendas. We all have our own buttons which, when pushed in the right way, can motivate us to move mountains. Recognise them and push them as often as you can.

After #50, my main reasons for learning my target language are #7, #18 and #24.

What are yours?

Why not tick the ones which are most appropriate for you? Are any of your reasons missing from the list? If so, add them on. They are all important.

Once you have identified all the reasons for learning your target language, you can then weigh them up against the time and effort necessary to do so. You are then in a position to ask yourself 'Is it worth it?'

If the answer is yes, you're on the right track.

Short-term Goals

Once you've identified your specific long-term goal, you can sit back and relax knowing a major part of your language learning project has been put into place.

But don't get too comfy. There's plenty more to be done.

Your Goal is of fundamental importance. It is your guiding star. It clearly identifies where you're are going and why you want to get there. But paradoxically, your Goal can also be a problem. If you spend too much time thinking about it, it can seem too big, too difficult or too much of a challenge for you to succeed.

This is due to the clear contrast of where you want to eventually be with where you are now. It's a vast difference—a huge step that you feel you are never going to be able to manage. Obviously, you can't eat an elephant in one bite and you can't do a 10,000-piece jigsaw puzzle in one afternoon.

This is where the power of little-by-little comes in. If you make sure you are getting a little bit nearer to your Goal every day, your eventual success is guaranteed. It's a mathematical certainty.

To do this, it is useful to set yourself a series of short-term goals—goals which are also **specific but much more attainable.**

If you're doing a marathon, you don't spend your time thinking about the finishing line. The finishing line is miles away and focussing on that isn't going to do you any good at all. So instead you focus on the traffic lights up ahead—they're not too far away at all. You can easily get to them. Then once you've reached the traffic lights, there's that parked yellow van up ahead. That's not too far, either. Then after that it's the tree, or the corner, or the statue or whatever. They're all short-term goals you can easily cope with.

Thus, after setting your long-term Goal, you can start to think about your short to medium goals: your monthly goal, your weekly goal, even your daily goal. These make the whole process much more palatable. We will be looking at different ways of setting up these easier goals in the following chapters.

Your Goal Diary

The most important book you'll ever own regarding achieving your target language objective is not your target-language dictionary, nor is it your *Teach Yourself...* book. It's not even this book! The most important book you'll ever have has not even been written yet. That's because you are going to write it. It's your *Goal Diary*.

Your Goal Diary is where you set down all the important things you need to collect along your journey towards your destination to achieve your chosen level in your target language.

Your Goal Diary will serve as an organiser, a way of setting down your objectives, your chosen pieces of your puzzle, your study timetable, your successes, your achievements and a way of storing all the positive emotions you will experience during your linguistic journey.

You begin by writing down your objective and then reinforcing it with all the reasons you have for wanting to get there. Don't be tempted to write what you're supposed to. Write the truth, or as close to the truth as possible. This list can be adjusted as necessary later on.

The next thing is to start writing down all the things you can do to help yourself on your journey—what I call the Pieces of the Puzzle. Some of them will be one-offs such as acquiring a Frequency Dictionary while others will be actions you can carry out every day. We'll be looking at these in the next chapter.

After that, you'll be setting down testament to all the progress you make— all the breakthroughs, discoveries and realisations you'll have. You'll need these when your motivation is running low.

Finally, you'll record all the positive emotional experiences you'll have: all the nobler positive feelings such as hope, excitement and pride.

All these you'll set down not for your own personal entertainment but for your own personal defence. Defence from an old enemy who is as persistent as anything you can come up with. His name is General Futility. We'll be meeting him in chapter 13.

With previous persevering projects, I kept my Diary on paper. But for some reason, for the first time with this project I decided to try keeping a note of everything on my phone. It's always handy. I can make a note of something whenever I like. I can even attach photos or links which is useful. It's always there for reference or inspiration and if I lose my phone it's all backed up in some mysterious place called the Cloud. But whether your Goal Diary is real or virtual, use it. We will be constantly revisiting your Goal Diary in future chapters.

Questions

1. What is your language learning goal?

2. What are your reasons for achieving it?

3. Is it worth it?

4. How are you going to know when you've achieved it?

5. How are you going to measure it?

6. When are you going to start?

7. When is your deadline?

8. What are your short-term goals?

9. When and from where are you going to get your Goal Diary?

·

The Pieces of the Puzzle

"Life is like a jigsaw puzzle. You have to see the whole picture, then put it together piece by piece!"

– Terry McMillan, American author

So far we've done a brief overview of the Sorites Principle, we've looked at the laws of language learning and we've established the importance both of having a clear goal and clear reasons for wanting it. Now we're going to look at the second step of the Sorites Principle—the 'how' part. The way we are going to learn our target language is by putting together all the 'Pieces of the Puzzle'.

Language learning is not just going through a few pages of a self-study book every day. There's much, much more to it than that.

There are many other activities you can do. Here I've listed the ones I've discovered and roughly divided them into four categories: Hardware, Software, Service Providers and Human Resources. Some of these I've regularly used myself. Some were recommended by others which I've tried but then decided were not for me. I'm by no means claiming that this list is complete and I know that the categories overlap in places. My objective is to get you to start considering what else you can to do improve your learning.

Hardware

Hardware is the stuff you can acquire and keep: physical objects you can have about you to help with your studies. There's plenty of it out there but think twice before you decide what to spend your money on.

- **Bilingual dictionary:** If you really want one, great. Go straight ahead. But don't be too ambitious. If you insist on buying one, get something modest you can carry easily. Big bilingual dictionaries might look impressive but are cumbersome. I have one. It's sitting on my bookshelf right now gathering dust. That's because I never use it. It's much easier to use a bilingual dictionary app or Google Translate instead.

- **Monolingual dictionary:** The advantage here is you have to work in your target language which is good practice. No use whatsoever if you're a beginner, very useful once you've reached elementary. Again, it's still easier to download a modest monolingual dictionary onto your device.

- **Frequency dictionary:** If your target language has one, so should you. It's nice to have the most important words you need to learn set out for you already in a user-friendly format. With just 500 of the most common words in your target language, you'll be able to understand 50% of normal language and be able to start communicating in predictable situations. Don't forget to add the important useful words you might need more than the average learner, such as wheelchair-access or diabetic. One of the problems of learning a minority language is there simply aren't the resources the bigger languages have. I couldn't find a Catalan frequency dictionary, not in the main bookshops nor on the internet and I couldn't find one to download either. You might have better luck.

- **Phrase books**. If you're the sort that likes phrase books, pick your favourite and covet it for life. I find a phrasebook to be something I'd buy but then hardly ever use. Facial expressions, pointing and advanced mime can communicate perfectly well what you want and have the job done before you can even get your phrasebook out of your bag. Rather than a phrasebook, again I'd use a translation app from my phone. They're quicker, more flexible and occupy less space. Using a combination of Google Translate, revision cards and a friendly native speaker to help with pronunciation, you can make your own personalised phrase collection in just a few days.

- **Grammar books**: If you really, really want to learn grammar, if it makes you happy, if it gives you that little buzz to understand the underlying laws of the language, then please, be my guest. But if just the very idea of studying grammar sends a shiver down your spine, then forget it. It's simply not necessary.

- **Course books**: If you're doing a course through a language school, you'll have an assigned Course Book. These are virtually useless to use by yourself as the teacher has a corresponding Teacher's Book which has all the information and instructions necessary for the Course Book to make any sense. If you have one, it's worth reading ahead and doing some preparation beforehand. This means you'll have an idea of what's in store for you. So when you get to that chapter, you'll already have some idea about the topic being presented in class and thus feel more confident and grasp it better. If you follow all the recommendations in this book, you'll soon find yourself the top student in your class and in a position to jump up to the next level if your language school will let you.[23]

- **Self-study books**: By all means, get one or two. It's interesting to see the difference in styles and inevitably you'll prefer some parts of one over the other and vice versa. Self-study books are good for giving you structure; they tell you what things you should learn which is a big help if you're feeling overwhelmed by the whole thing. Another advantage they have over anything you can load onto your phone is

---

23- You might like to consider getting the course book of the class above you so you can follow what they are doing while you're getting ready to make the jump.

you can write in them. You can underline, highlight and circle stuff. You can write notes in the margin and draw lewd diagrams for your own entertainment when necessary.

I bought two self-study books. I did at least a page a day for the first few months. But I eventually found I was getting enough things to learn from my daily use of my target language so I stopped. This is great news if you don't like self-study books—they're not compulsory but they can help.

- **Goal Diary**: Your goal diary could also be considered a piece of hardware, too.

- **Smartphone**: If you haven't gathered already, your smartphone is one of the most useful accessories to language learning money can buy. Not just because of the apps, the internet connection and the free international video calls. Your smartphone can also send you reminders for your regular language learning activities or can take photos of interesting texts you come across to be studied later at your convenience. It can also be used for reading e-books in your target language whenever you fancy, wherever you are. If you haven't got one yet, I'd strongly recommend you get one. If you don't like mobile phones because you don't like receiving calls and bothersome messages, you can always rip out the SIM card, deactivate all the alerts and just use it as a small handheld computer. You can start showing you're serious by setting the language of your phone to your target language.

- **Music with understandable lyrics**: Some people swear by this. If you're just starting, most likely you have no idea of what music is out there in your target language. When I was learning Spanish, I got recommended all sorts of stuff that I acquired and almost immediately binned as the induced nausea was intolerable.[24] But maybe I was just unlucky or have a sheltered taste in music. Nowadays it's easy to preview stuff on YouTube, Spotify or iTunes to know what you're letting yourself in for. Win friends and influence people by learning a popular song in your

---

24- I must point out that, since then, I have discovered lots of Spanish music that is excellent. Stuff I've liked so much I've paid good money for. It's just a question of exploring till you find something that entices your ear.

target language. How about learning the national anthem? (How about learning your national anthem while you're at it?)

- **Films etc.:** Part of your language learning programme is to enjoyably experience your target language. Watching a film or TV series is a very good way to achieve this. There are a few important recommendations about watching stuff on video which we'll be looking at later in chapter 8.

- **Literature:** Every language has its corresponding culture. You can't get to really know one without learning about the other. So it's a good idea to dip into it if you can. This doesn't mean you should start trying to read Shakespeare or the equivalent in your target language. Far from it. Any author from over two hundred years ago is going to be speaking in a style that is at best dated or at worst unintelligible. If you want to learn a language, at least go for something written recently. This is where your Language Forum comes in useful. Post a message asking for recommended reading, listening or watching. If you tell them your current reading, listening or viewing preferences, that will help them recommend something similar. You'll get dozens, if not hundreds, of different suggestions. Give preference to native authors. Harry Potter might be a gripping read but it'll do little to increase your cultural awareness of your target language.

- **Readers:** Did you know there exist simplified or 'graded' readers? These are books with all the complicated language filtered out of them, leaving a vocabulary base much easier to manage. They're shorter, too, and so less intimidating. What's more, some of them have helpful appendices with useful information, vocab and informative illustrations.

- **Bilingual books:** It was a jaw-dropping experience for the wife when she discovered there exist books printed in two languages: one language on the left-hand page and the same text in the second language printed on the right. If you like that sort of thing, great, but I tried them and I find it just makes me lazy. Instead of trying to understand the language, your eyes automatically flick to the opposite page. I call that cheating.

- **Kids' books:** Do not underestimate the usefulness of kids' story books. Even the books aimed at young children can serve you well. I can say this with authority because I've learnt lots from them. Kids' storybooks have two advantages: They have pictures to help you understand what you're reading about and they have simple plots. By this I mean there is no flipping back and forth in a timeframe or from one place to another which can be very confusing. Children's stories follow the main character from start to finish.[25]

And while we're on the subject, all children are brought up knowing children's songs and rhymes. It's part of their culture. If you learn some of these you'll practise chunking, you'll further develop your cultural awareness and you'll be a big hit the next time you meet your language exchange partner's younger family members.

- **Magazines**: You can now mail-order almost any magazine from any part of the world (or why not just read it online?). Tailor-made to match your personal interests, you can find articles in your target language from amateur astronomy to car maintenance. If it's a subject that interests you, then you're more likely to spend time reading it.

- **Comics**: When I was learning French at school, my father got me a load of Asterix the Gaul comics (in French, of course) which I thought were great. The advantages are obvious: They have wonderful illustrations, they tend to have practical dialogue as opposed to verbose descriptions and the stories are fun. There are all sorts of comic in all sorts of languages. Explore, select and add them to your language learning repertoire.

Of all the activities, **reading for pleasure** is one of my favourites. I now get immense satisfaction from being able to read without hardly needing to consult Google Translate. But even so, I can clearly remember struggling with even the simplest of texts. The obvious progress is reassuringly satisfying. It's nice to match the level of your reading material to your language level. But it's not obligatory. What is important is to match your reading activity to your level.

25- I read the complete set of *Les tres bessones* (The Triplets) by the Catalan writer/illustrator Roser Capdevilla. I also got hooked to the *Four and a Half Friends* books in Catalan (*Quatre amics i mig*) written by Joachim Friedrich. They're a set of stories similar to Enid Blyton's *Famous Five* but up to date and better.

If you're a beginner, trying to read a newspaper or magazine article is not going to be easy. It can lead to frustration which results in demotivation. You are best to accept you're not going to understand everything but you can start to understand something. Limit yourself to scanning just one page, identifying what words you do understand with a pencil. You could also look for any frequently repeated words or groups of words and learn what they mean.

Reading doesn't have to be synonymous with 'understanding every word'. Allow yourself to not know and to skip unknown words or make an educated guess at what they mean and move on. Don't worry. There'll be plenty of time to go back and check what the correct meaning is if you want to.

- **Games**: There are gamified apps like Duolingo but I'm not talking about these. I'm talking about real games you can play with a friend or two who are also interested in practising. You can mail-order games in your target language (e.g. Monopoly or Trivial Pursuit) and enjoy many happy hours learning expressions such as 'It's your turn', 'Pass me the dice' and 'I saw that, you cheating swine!' Games are great because they allow you to 'play' with the language and relax a little. Check out Amazon or your nearest friendly local supplier for language learning games.

- **Revision cards**: These are really, really important. Following Law 16, you should be revising several times a day. We'll be looking more at revision later in chapter 7.

- **Post-its**: You can use sticky bits of coloured paper for reminding you to do stuff like 'Revise now' or you can label objects in your target language helping you remember what they're called. There are a few useful rules for using Post-its which we'll look at in chapter 10.

- **Past exam papers**: If one of your goals is to sit an exam, it would be a great idea to do a few past papers. You might be able to download them for free or buy books full of past exam examples. Ask your forum for advice.

- **Pen and paper**: I still remember the berating a university professor gave one of my colleagues 30 years ago: "Call yourself a student and you dare turn up to one of my lectures without a bloody pen?!" You need to be constantly writing stuff down until you can get it onto a revision card and firmly ingrained into your long-term memory. It sounds obvious, yet so often we forget.

Software

Some of the most useful tools to help me on my language learning journey were software. Not physical stuff but apps, data and webpages all available at the touch of a button.

- **Translation apps:** As I've already mentioned, I found Google Translate to be one of my most useful tools. I reckon I must have used it every single day. Unlike a dictionary, you can type in the whole phrase and get a complete answer. Admittedly, some of the translations can be a bit dodgy and the accompanying simulated pronunciation still has much room for improvement. But for ease and simplicity, it's definitely my first point of reference. Furthermore, I just love the way you can point your camera at your target text and the app automatically 'translates' the image into English. Brilliant for restaurant menus, signposts and bedtime reading, though it doesn't work well in dim lighting.

- **Revision apps:** Another top tool was my revision app. I used **AnkiApp** because I found it to be the most flexible. In some ways, revision (or Flashcard) apps are limited in that you can only put on them what the app allows and you can only have one visible at a time, whereas for revising I find spreading the cards out on a table in front of me much more satisfying.

- **Study apps:** There are lots of free apps that will teach you step by step your new language. Current popular ones are Babbel, Memrise, Duolingo and Busuu, but I'm sure that right now someone somewhere is about to launch one that is even better.

- **Websites:** One of my most used websites was exclusively dedicated to verb conjugation in Catalan (verbs.cat). Type in your verb and it immediately gives you all the conjugations, pointing out the regular, semi-regular and irregular cases. It even had a revision mode feature, which was nice. Do a search for learning your target language. You might be surprised by how many sites there are set up by altruistic individuals offering to help you learn their language absolutely free. Some of them are brilliantly creative, some of them have room for improvement and some are just plain weird. But they are all potentially pieces of your puzzle. Take half an hour to sit down and explore. Make a note of the websites that most appeal to you so that once your head starts swirling with so many different and bedazzling new fountains of knowledge, you'll be able to find your way back to the ones you want to stick with. I've included a short list of general language learning websites as part of the recommended references in the 'Sources' section at the back.

- **YouTube:** An excellent source for tutorials, vlogs, presentations, lectures and all sorts of videos that can help you learn your chosen language.

It is now so easy to make a video and post it on the web, it seems everyone is doing it, including language teachers. Just search for 'learning Italian' or 'Hindi tutorial'. There is a trove of stuff. It's all for free and most of it is very good. Admittedly, some of it is a bit amateur, but hey, what the hell? These people are making an effort so you get to see free lessons online. It's a good idea to pay special attention to the ones on pronunciation. No amount of reading can beat a video demonstrating the more challenging parts of pronouncing your new language.

- **Skype:** If you don't know how to do it yet, get someone to teach you. It'll come in very useful for talking to people on the other side of the planet for free.

Service Providers

Here we're talking about people who'll do things for you if you give them enough money.

- **Local language schools:** Discover them. Check them out. Visit them, virtually and physically, even if you've no intention of enrolling in a course. Such places often have notice boards, clubs, information, all sorts of stuff that might come in useful. They'll probably do you a level assessment for free, too.

- **Online courses**: These come in all forms: some lovingly created by altruistic enthusiasts to help you achieve what they did, others lovingly created to relieve you of as much money as possible. If you're one of those who feel you have to be financially invested in your project to guarantee motivation, the BBC have a fine selection of quality courses, as do 'Michel Thomas', 'Teach Yourself' and 'Assimil', to name just a few. Again, do a search for top online courses for your target language or ask your forum group. But don't forget, if you follow all the suggestions in this book you should easily be able to learn your language without ever having to spend a penny.[26]

- **Private teachers**: A good private, one-to-one teacher is worth his or her weight in gold. As a language learner, you need motivation to speak in your new language but you also need to be checked, corrected, guided and challenged. It's difficult to do all of this on your own. In a perfect world, a good language exchange partner can help but they're unlikely to prepare tasks for you or be at your beck and call for months at a time. Private teachers are. Most give a free introductory get-to-know-me session. Take advantage of this and try a few. Pick the teacher you're happiest with.

- **Private tutors**: Tutors are similar to teachers but don't have so much training. They're just normal people who are interested in helping you practice your target language while earning a bit on the side. They're cheaper but simply don't have the experience a trained teacher has. For higher levels, this isn't necessarily a problem.

- **Exams:** You don't have to study a language course in a school or college to sit an official exam. There's nothing to stop you from sitting an exam independently. It's exactly what I did. Exams are a great objective to set yourself. Once you've registered for the exam, you'll feel that little tingle of excitement.

- **International radio and TV**: From the day I started to the day I finished my six-month venture, I listened to the news in my target language

---

26- Not including broadband connection, roaming charges, transport costs to meetings, private classes, beer and coffee money, romantic dinners, flights and hotels. But what the hell? You can't take it with you, can you?

every commute to and from work. That's almost 50 minutes in total every day. You can listen to a staggering amount of radio stations via internet. Most cities have a local radio station. Google 'radio [insert name of city here] online', sit back and absorb.

- You can also get international TV through sites such as YouTube, FilmOn or Streema. See chapter 8.

- **Low cost flights and Airbnb:** As I mentioned before, you don't have to live in the country of your target language. But in this ever-shrinking world in which we live, it just gets easier and more affordable to travel. Treat yourself to a weekend away. If you can go alone, all the better. I went inter-railing round Europe on my own and met loads of people. I went to France with the wife for a week and hardly spoke to anyone else. If you're on your own, you're much more likely to get real conversation practice. This can be exciting or demoralising, depending on who you encounter. It could well be one of the most challenging activities you can to do. It's so far out of your comfort zone it seems unreachable. Bite the bullet by embracing embarrassment and losing your identity for a while. This can only happen if you make the effort to carry out the MOST EFFECTIVE language activity and have real conversations with real speakers in a real context.

Human Resources

Languages are for communicating with other people and the best activities you can do to learn most effectively involve doing it with other people.

- **Native speakers in your area:** Geography is no longer a problem for language learning. Even if you've never ventured further than your hometown, it's now perfectly possible there's someone nearby who's a native speaker of your target language. When they find out you're interested in their language, people open up and can be very hospitable. Don't be afraid to ask for their help and support. They might say no. If they do, you've lost nothing. But if they say yes, you are gaining practice time, valuable direct experience, peer support and possibly a great friend.

- **Local language exchange groups**: All of the above advantages but without the embarrassment of having to ask. They can be very 'hit and miss'. I tried out a few different groups with some very mixed results.

- **Cultural associations**. I was surprised to learn only about 40% of the members of the American Society of Barcelona are Americans. Being a native is not a requisite. If your neighbourhood is lucky enough to have a French/Brazilian/Chinese cultural society, don't hesitate to join up and join in. Partly social, partly networking, they talk about anything vaguely connected with their group and are happy with any excuse for a party. If you're a higher level, these groups can be much more stimulating than the 'Oh, hi, my name's Kevin. Where are you from?' language exchange sort.

- **Study Buddies**. Going it alone can be tough. If you have someone to share the journey with, all the better. You can help each other, have friendly competition, be a shoulder for the other to cry on. If you have the opportunity to join up with someone who also shares your Goal, then that's brilliant. You don't even have to study together; just sharing experiences can be nice.

- **Accountability partners**. Your best friend, favourite aunt or coach might not be interested in learning your target language, but they might be interested in helping you to persevere with it. Get them to promise to hit you on the head with a chair if you don't stick to your language learning plan. The thought of having to pick the splinters out can be a great motivator.

- **Praise Donors**: Similar to accountability partners but with fewer chairs and more 'well-done's'.

- **Forums**: Online groups that talk about what you're interested in. Great for getting good ideas and information. Forums can point you in the right direction to whatever you're looking for and save you time, frustration and embarrassment. From the best online courses, to the best films to watch, to the best expressions to learn, they provide really good inside information.

- One good example is **HiNative**, which describes itself as a global platform for language learners where you can ask and answer questions about language and culture with native speakers around the world. At the moment they have forums on 110 languages. Without fear of ridicule you can select your target language and then send in your questions such as 'What does this expression mean?' or 'How do people really say hello?' or even 'Where's the best place to eat in [insert name of town here]?' It also comes in a convenient app, which I think is lovely. It's like having the whole world in one tiny icon.

- **Language exchange partners**: Having a friend who is happy to help you learn their language in exchange for you helping them learn yours is a great way to study. Language exchanges are free and can be fun. On the downside, half of your time is spent helping them learn your language which might be taking up your valuable study time. What's more, your exchange partner is unlikely to have you as a priority in their life. Expect changes of timetables, postponements and last-minute cancellations. If what you need is reliability, consider a teacher or tutor.

- **Dating partners**: One of the advantages (or disadvantages) to interpersonal exchanges is physical attraction. If you're free and single and looking for a bit of extracurricular linguistic practice, there's no harm what-so-ever in dating a speaker of your target language. Not only will you have fun practising your new language in circumstances hither to unimaginable, but you'll also (just like Henry XIII and Catherine of Aragon) be bringing two cultures closer together and thus, in one small way, increase the level of international peace and harmony.

Questions

- How many of these pieces do you usually use?

- How many of these pieces are you overlooking?

- Can you think of any other resources or activities?

- Which of these activities could you do every day?

- Who can help you?

- Where can you find a few spare minutes every morning, every midday, every afternoon, every evening and every night to put a couple of pieces into place?

Perseverance

"Little by little you fill the sink and drop by drop you fill the barrel"

– Catalan Proverb[27]

So you've set your goal and picked a range of activities you can do. Lovely!

The final step of the plan is to carry out each activity as often as you can every day until you reach your goal. To the uninitiated, this might sound like no big deal. When you set off on the language learning adventure, it is quite easy to start with. It's all fresh and shiny. But inevitably, the shininess wears off. What started as something you looked forwards to starts to become a chore.

This can happen for several reasons such as running out of willpower, the feeling of general futility or procrastination. You might start to suffer from a feeling that you're not making satisfactory progress, or that your chosen

---

27- *"De mica en mica s'omple la pica i de gota en gota s'omple la bota."* It rhymes better in Catalan.

activities are a waste of time. You might even feel that although all these different ways of learning might be very well for most people, you are different and so they're not for you.

Far from being different, this sort of thinking is what most of us go through at one point or another. We all encounter periods of doubt and uncertainty. Will it work? Can I do it? Is it worth it? Am I wasting my time?

Yes, it will. Yes, you can. Yes, it is. No, you're not wasting your time.

Just like the grains of sand being added to the heap, one grain makes hardly any difference at all. Nevertheless, if you continue to add another and then another, as often as you can, you will inevitably get the heap of sand you were aiming for. It's just a question of perseverance.

The average six-year-old has an active vocabulary (words they are able to reproduce) of about two and a half thousand words and a passive vocabulary (words they can recognise) of about twenty thousand. That means an average of learning just over one active word a day and nine passive ones. As an adult, you are capable of beating these numbers easily. Conservative estimates talk about adult students learning at least five new active words a day. This is still a low figure. Language-learning experts can learn ten to twenty new words a day. But even if we stick to just five, if you had started to study a year ago you'd now have a vocabulary base of over 1,800[28] easily enough to make yourself understood in most normal situations.

But this simple explanation is not going to be enough to keep you going for the months and months needed to achieve your goal. I know this because I've been there.

28- . This is assuming all the words are all new. It is also nice to know all languages have some vocabulary in common with English, mostly due to English borrowing words and lending others in return. In German, a glass is *'ein glas'*, in French a table is *'une table'*, in Italian an umbrella is *'un ombrello'* and in Dutch a cow is *'een koe'*. It's not unreasonable to suppose you already know hundreds of words in your newly chosen language before you even open your first book and that's not even including universal words such as taxi, hotel, guitar, okay, bikini, pizza, meter, coffee, sauna, nylon, chocolate, Coca Cola, Big Mac, iPhone and Ferrari.

Not only do you need a few motivational words and a kick up the bum, you also need a whole set of perseverance tools you can rely on daily to keep you going when the going gets tough. These are the key to the Sorites Principle. These are what makes persevering possible.

I've divided these perseverance tools into eight categories: Prizes, Progress, Passion, Peer Pressure, Pointers, Periodic Actions, Patience and Positivity. These are the eight 'P's of perseverance and if you can learn how to harness the power of each one, you'll find that perseverance is so easy you'll start to wonder why it was you weren't able to do it before.

Consider the following questions and then we'll start with the first one.

Questions

- What have you achieved through perseverance?

- What were the reasons you were able to manage it?

- What projects did you fail to persevere with?

- What were the reasons you failed?

- Who do you know who has recently learnt a new language?

- Do you know how they managed it?

- If you had started studying six months ago, learning something every day, how many words would you have learnt by now?

Prizes

"Learning is a treasure that will follow its owner everywhere."

– *Chinese Proverb*

What Casinos Do Best

The gambling industry is very clever. It has to be. If I were to open a building to the general public with a large sign saying, 'Please come in and give me all your money in exchange for some flashing lights and jiggly bells' I don't think I'd get very far. But the whole casino setup, from the attractive décor to the attractive croupiers, is carefully designed to do just that: to lure in potential customers and persuade them to part with their cash.

Consider the slot machines, or the 'one-armed bandits' as my family calls them. They are the main income for casinos, providing well over half a casino's revenue. They're almost magical entities. They cast a spell over us. They are designed to make the likelihood of you choosing to try your luck as high as possible. This is achieved by rewarding the insertion of your coin with pretty lights, entertaining sounds, dynamic visuals, the occasional small win and the more occasional tantalising near miss of a huge jackpot. None of these rewards cost the casino much money. They are trivial. But they are enough to maintain the player's motivation to keep inserting coins.

You might be doubtful of this. You might say it's the chance to win the $10,000 jackpot that keeps them going. Maybe. But what if, instead of a pretty, twinkly machine, we had a solid black box—a slab of grim metal with no lights, no sounds, no visuals. Nothing but a slot. Yet you are told with complete certainty the chance of winning on this machine is exactly the same as the flashy, jingly ones. You insert your coin and if you win, it dumps the winnings at your feet, but if you lose…nothing, there is no reaction at all. Just the sound of your coin disappearing into the innards of the big black slab. Would you be enticed to put your money in it? Given that regular slot-machine players spend hours on the same machine, how long do you think they'd keep shoving coins into the unresponsive black box? 'Not very long at all' is my guess. The little rewards of lights and sounds make all the difference.

The machine is designed to make you want to put in your next coin. There is no option for increasing the amount. There's no pressure to increase your wager to, let's say, $100 in one go. It's a regular drip, drip, drip of coins. The $100 input will be reached, but slowly and steadily over time. For you, the punter, playing with 'just one coin' is morally acceptable. Nothing to flinch at. But if the machine tried to get too much out of you too soon… Ouch! Losing $100 or $1000 in just one go is too much. It creates a negative response. It jeopardises the continuation of our behaviour. Asking for too much can break the spell.

What can we learn from casinos?

Two things:

1. Small rewards are enough to motivate our actions

2. If we desire a long period of activity, we just need focus on rewarding the next action required.

So what has this to do with learning a language?

To learn your language, you need to carry out a whole range of activities such as reading, listening, conversation practice and revising (your pieces of the puzzle). Often, you will encounter resistance to these activities. If you can find a way of keeping the activity small and simple and a way of rewarding your behaviour, of giving yourself a prize every now and then, it can make all the difference.

When I say 'prize', I'm not talking about big things like rewarding yourself a fortnight in Paris once you've learned French. Promising ourselves a big reward (such as holidays, cars or jewellery) for reaching our final goal can have an adverse effect on our perseverance. We see everything as large and far away. As we will see later in the section on Patience, focussing on things that are large and far away, things that (for the moment) are unattainable, can cause us anxiety, producing the sense of being overwhelmed.

Thinking of a huge prize for finally reaching a huge goal which must be achieved by putting in a huge amount of time and effort doesn't work. We are much more likely to find ourselves saying "It's too big, it's too difficult. I'm never going to be fluent. I'm wasting my time. It's never going to happen."

Big prizes for big achievements don't work. Small prizes for small achievements do.

What counts as a small prize? Practically anything that gives you that small dose of dopamine.[29] For myself, I use tea, stretching and crossing stuff off. I'll promise myself that once I've listened to a podcast then I'll have a cuppa. I'll study or write for an hour and then give myself a break—maybe do a bit of stretching or let the dog take me for a short drag up the road. I'll do my Skype language exchange for an hour, then I can cross it off my list of things-to-do-today which feels nicely satisfying. It's not rocket science, but it's enough. They make all the difference and language learning app designers know this.

29- Dopamine is a chemical released in the brain that affects our behaviour. It is a 'feel good' molecule that serves to reward and reinforce certain kinds of behaviour like eating, drinking and putting coins into slot machines. Getting a small release of dopamine feels nice. Getting a large one feels even nicer. Drugs such as cocaine, nicotine and heroin chemically induce the release of dopamine in large amounts. This is why they are so addictive.

Gamified Apps

I was recommended Duolingo by a friend who was already using it to learn Spanish. I thought I'd investigate. I was told it won iPhone App of the Year in 2013 and Google's Best of the Best in 2014, and with millions of downloads already at the time of writing, it must be doing something right. It all sounded quite promising so I thought I'd give it a go.

I liked it.

First of all, it's free which is great. "Why pay for it when you can get it for nothing?" could have been the legend on our family coat of arms, if we'd had one. I suppose it's what you get for being a Yorkshireman.

I liked its design. It's clean, simple, colourful and fun. When you download it, it comes up as a little bright green icon with the face of a cute owl. It presents language learning in the form of a game. You can choose to start with the basics and go along completing stages or you can do a level (or 'placement') test, which I think is nice and only takes about five minutes. If you think the level is easy then you can take a fast route by taking a mini test to skip it.

Some of the computer simulated pronunciations are a bit dodgy. For example, when I did the test to see how good my English was, the word 'corner' was distinctly pronounced as 'corn-war' which isn't how I pronounce it at all. 'Dog' was pronounced 'dawlg' which I'm sure shouldn't have an 'l' in it. After five minutes of questions, I was told my level of English was 74%. And that was getting everything right. Obviously I needed to try harder.

One final thing: I used Duolingo to study my target language for a period of four months, but as the time wore on, I found it becoming less and less interesting. The process of learning was the same all the way through. There was nothing new in its format. The exercises became unimaginatively predictable. In short, its shininess wore off.

Nevertheless, for what it is—a free language learning app—I would definitely recommend it as one of your tools to put in your language learning toolbox.

These gamified apps are a good way of building up your vocabulary, but language learning is so much more than just learning to recognise words. You need to be able to read, write, speak and listen. How can we apply the idea of prizes to these? One answer is to use stars.

The Star Chart

When I say star chart, I'm not talking about the sort that say you're about to meet a tall dark handsome stranger. No. As far as your language studies go, a star chart refers to a great way of motivating yourself to do a little of whatever it is you want to be doing by using those simple but effective 'Gold Merit Stars'. You remember them, don't you? The ones your teacher used to stick in your exercise book for writing something legible or drawing a cow that looked like a cow. They made you feel great, didn't they?[30]

The principle of the Star Chart is exactly the same. But instead of awarding yourself a star for drawing a cow, you give yourself one for drawing a cow and then labelling its anatomy correctly in your chosen language or whatever language learning activity you've set yourself.

A Star Chart is simply a monthly calendar, or a sheet of paper with a 7 by 5 grid. Each box represents a day of the month (with a few left over). For every day you do your desired activity such as studying, having a language exchange or listening to an audiobook, you give yourself the wondrous prize of a small sticky piece of gold foil in the shape of a star— or a circle, diamond or butterfly. Whatever your local stationers has that tickles your fancy.

The Star Chart works not only because it provides that little reward for doing 'whatever-it-is'. It also serves as a simple reminder or prompt (more about these in chapter 10). If you stick your Star Chart somewhere, you're going to see it every day and it will help focus your attention on what you have to do.

30- That was the dopamine.

It does this in two ways. Firstly, due to its mere physical presence and secondly due to the potential reward of getting your next star. So set yourself a target. How many times are you going to study or practise each month? Eight? Twelve? Sixteen? How about every day? Pick your realistic target and go for it.

Mon	Tue	Wed	Thu	Fri	Sat	Sun
		1	2	3	4	5
6	7	8	9	10	11	12
13	14	15	16	17	18	19
20	21	22	23	24	25	26
27	28	29	30	31		

Fig 1. Star Chart

A little reminder and reward might be just what you need. But if you need to stretch yourself a bit more then there's more to come.

How about giving yourself points instead of stars?

Points Are Prizes Too

Another motivator I remember from my old school days is the idea of house points. If you did something good, you got a house point. If you did something truly spectacular, you got a whole bundle of them. And if they're good enough for Hogwarts, they're good enough for you.

Instead of (or in addition to) using stars, at the end of the day you give yourself points depending on how much you achieved. Clearly, ten minutes of studying is not as good as two hours and two pages of reading isn't as good as two chapters, so here you can motivate yourself to do more of your desired activity by evaluating it and writing it on your chart.

10 minutes working from your study book = 1 point

10 minutes of reading in your target language = 2 points

10 minutes of watching or listening to a recording = 3 points

10 minutes of practising your target language out loud = 4 points

10 minutes of improvised conversation with yourself = 5 points

10 minutes of conversation with your teacher / language partner = 7 points

10 minutes of real conversation in a real situation = 10 points

You can then add up your weekly total and note it at the end of each row. This way you can compete against yourself by trying to beat the score of the previous week.

It adds that little bit of worthwhileness to your studies. If you're tired and thinking about packing it in for the day, knowing that giving it another ten minutes will get you those extra points might just make the difference you need to keep at it.

Crossing Stuff Off

If shiny stars and points are not your cup of tea, how about using another simple method that's worked for me for years: the simple satisfaction of crossing stuff off. Every evening as part of my bedtime routine (more about the importance of routines in chapter 11) I write down my 'things-to-do-tomorrow' list. Then the following day, every time I carry out one of my things-to-do, I cross it off with satisfaction. It feels good.

A friend of mine called Ruth has a similar system, but she's an Excel[31] fanatic. She has all of her 'to-do' list on a spreadsheet: calls to be made,

---

31- Excel is the Microsoft spreadsheet programme.

emails to send, stuff to buy, people to see, etc. She's studying Turkish, so her Turkish classes, homework periods and language exchange Skypes are also included. Each has a scheduled time and accompanying notes and observations. She showed me it. It filled up a whole screen. Her trick was to change the background colour of each row from white to green once it had been done. She also had a system for prioritising tasks using yellow, orange and red. Stuff that had to be postponed was cut and pasted onto the appropriate day's corresponding spreadsheet. But her prize was to turn each row green, one by one throughout the day, until her whole sheet was green. Then she could pack up and go home. "Seeing that sheet of solid green at the end of the day—that makes me feel great. I know I've had a good day," she says with a smile. Turning a row green is Ruth's small prize. It's all she needs to keep her going.

So how about setting out your list of the little activities you'd like to carry out tomorrow on paper, a spreadsheet, your smartphone or the back of your hand and then spend the day happily crossing them off?

Recognition & Praise

Imagine you've just had one of those days where you felt truly inspired to give your home a jolly good seeing to.

You tidied, wiped, cleaned, swept, hoovered and polished until the place was gleaming. You've just sat down with a well-deserved martini when your best-beloved staggers in, dumps their bag on the table with one hand while grabbing a beer from the fridge with the other, collapses on the sofa and, while flicking through the channels, absentmindedly enquires what's for dinner.

It's all a bit of a disappointment, isn't it? All that effort and for what? A "This place is looking clean and tidy. Well done!" would be appreciated. Just a little recognition would make all the difference.

The truth is a little recognition really does make all the difference.

Recognising your own ability also counts. So you've been studying basic Hebrew, Hindu or Hungarian for a month now. You can count to a hundred, have simple conversations about, names, jobs and the weather and conjugate the verb 'to be'. Well done. Acknowledge your progress by adding your basic language level to your C.V. or your LinkedIn skills section. The day I added 'Catalan' to my profile I felt quite excited. It was like some very small and personal graduation ceremony. So print it on your next business card if you like but accept your progress as a permanent ability and include it in any description of who you are. And stating your level as 'beginner' is being perfectly modest, after all, you're only going to get better from here on, aren't you?

We also respond to social rewards from others such as recognition, praise and admiration. If you can get someone to recognise and praise your efforts, you'll feel better about carrying them out next time. We'll be looking at how to get the practical as well as the psychological help of other people in Peer Pressure, chapter 9.

Punishments

Punishments are also a sort of prize but with a negative value.

If you think the idea of giving yourself a prize for studying is a bit lame, how about giving yourself a punishment if you don't? Some people respond better to punishments than prizes. So you could say to yourself that if you don't do your homework you won't go out with your mates, or you won't watch your favourite TV series, or you'll have your deep-pan oven-pizza but without the extra cheese and chillies. If you're not sure you can trust yourself to carry out a punishment, delegate the responsibility to a trusted flatmate or family member. Make them promise if you don't carry out your language learning activity then they'll burn your signed copy of *Dark Side of the Moon* or confiscate the control to the telly for twenty-four hours. Your masochistic imagination is the limit.

I suggest you try playing around with these ideas of giving yourself little prizes or punishments for (not) completing your chosen language learning activities. Experiment with them. Find out what works for you and what doesn't. Tweak them. Play around with them. Adapt them to your needs and make them your own.

Remember, these ideas work not only because they are providing you with a simple reward every day, but they also help draw your attention to your language learning. Your prizes serve as a reminder and a prompt to focus on them. The more you focus on your regular daily activities, the more time you're going to spend on them. And that's great because doing a little regularly every day is the best way to make solid steady progress.

The subject of progress is extremely important. So important that it needs a chapter all to itself. So let's do that after you've answered the following questions.

Questions

- In what ways do you reward your desired daily behaviours?

- Do you know of anyone who already uses small prizes to motivate themselves?

- Do you respond more to prizes or punishments? Can you think of an example?

- What other small prizes (or punishments) can you think of that might also work?

- Which of these could work best for you?

- What would you need to do in order to start?

- When are you going to do it?

Case Study 2: Charlie

Charlie never intended to learn a foreign language but a combination of factors changed his mind quite quickly. Firstly, just before his fortieth birthday, his fiancée left him, literally running off with another man to New York (apparently they'd met doing the London marathon). It was totally out of the blue. He was left in an empty house with too many memories, feeling 'small and confused'. But then there was a silver lining. Charlie was the U.K. Sales Director for an international chemical company. Two weeks after becoming involuntarily single, he was assured there was going to be a job opportunity coming up in eight months for head of Sales of Western Europe and he could be a top candidate. The only problem was it was in Cologne (Köln) and although English was the working language of the company, being able to speak German was considered to be an important requirement. His ex-fiancée would never have agreed to it. But that was before and now things were different. He decided a new job in a new country in a new house full of new memories was just what he needed. He went for it. Charlie decided he was going to learn German in eight months.

- Straight away he had a clear goal with a clear timeframe and a few clear reasons for achieving it.

- He also found the more he focussed on his language learning, the less time he spent focussing on his ex-fiancée. "It was almost like having therapy." He said later, "I'd no control over what she did, but I could control how I reacted. It was as if studying was my way of getting my own back. She wouldn't have approved of it at all. It was all to do with me and nothing to do with her."

- Charlie started with an advantage. He'd studied a bit of German at school (GCSE) and so was soon able to remember the basics.

- He was able to get the go-ahead to organise himself private German classes (one to one) four days a week through his company.

- He organised a morning routine. He'd get up early and watch 20 minutes of news in German while having breakfast. He'd then study for 40 minutes which he divided into two parts. The first half he spent doing exercises from the course book he used with his German teacher. His second half was to read. He printed off anything he found interesting (in German) on the internet and read it three times. Once to learn vocabulary, second to consolidate meaning and then finally out loud for pronunciation.

- Charlie also discovered he had a lot of free time in the evenings. He set up an evening routine. He'd spend an hour going over his notes and making revision cards and then try something more relaxing like watching German TV or a film with subtitles, always taking notes about anything new or confusing.

- He tried to listen to German music but discovered that most of Germany seemed to listen to music in English.

- After a couple of months, he started having language exchanges via Skype. In his first two weeks he talked to eleven people (some stranger than others). He settled on two: a young man from Frankfurt who was in a similar situation (moving to England for work) though his English was already very good and a middle-aged woman from Vienna who had an English-speaking grandson.

- At the height of his studying, with his classes and his language exchanges Charlie was getting in over six hours of speaking practice a week.

- After four months studying, he decided to spend a week visiting Cologne and the neighbouring towns where he made an effort to engage people in German and resist everyone's attempts to practise their English with him. He said the reaction people had when they found out he wanted to improve his German was truly heart-warming and he was made to feel something of a minor celebrity in his small hotel. That was when he met Tania.

- Tania turned out to be just what Charlie needed. She spoke a little English, but as he was keen to practise German it became their default language. He kept in contact with her after his week in Cologne on FaceTime and he was very pleased that even if he didn't get the job he was after, all his studying had been for something after all.

As he had been correctly led to believe, the position of European manager came up in November and he had a small joint flat-warming / New Year's Eve party in a frost-covered Cologne with Tania and a few friends. As he says, "If I'd have been told 12 months before that the following year I'd be living and working in Germany, being able to talk in German and dating a German girl, I'd have told them they were barking mad!"

Questions

- How many ways was Charlie motivated?

- What were the pieces of his language learning puzzle?

- What did he do to help persevere?

- If you had been Charlie, would you have done anything differently?

- Regarding language learning, is there anything else you find noteworthy about Charlie's experience?

Progress

"One language sets you in a corridor for life. Two languages open every door along the way."

–Frank Smith, psycholinguist

Jerry

A friend of mine has a hamster called Jerry. He's a fat little fellow (Jerry, not my friend) which is surprising considering the amount of time he spends on his little wheel. I've never seen a rodent exercise so much. I don't know what goes on inside his little hamster head but considering the ferocity of Jerry's relationship with his wheel, it wouldn't surprise me at all if it was some sort of misdirected form of sexual gratification. Or maybe it satisfies some deep emotional need, a way of venting 'cage-rage'? Maybe I should get a big wheel myself and try it out. But regardless of what Jerry's motives are for spending what seems like forever trundling away on a cylindrical piece of yellow plastic, what he hasn't figured out is he's not making any real progress. He might have the sensation of making some headway into his chosen endeavour but he is sadly misguided.[32]

Unfortunately, Jerry is not alone.

From time to time, I come across people who suffer from the same delusion. They have their own little activity that they busy themselves with, but without making any progress whatsoever.

I've known people who 'dieted' without ever losing weight. I've known people who 'studied' a language for years without being able to hold the simplest of conversations. They attended classes, bought material, watched videos but never seem to actually improve.

Maybe I'm being a little uncharitable, but how often have you felt that you've made a substantial step forward by just having bought a book on a subject? Or having downloaded an app? Or by just attending a few classes?

'Hang on!' you might protest, 'Attending classes is progressing, isn't it?' I don't want to disappoint you but signing a bit of paper, handing over the cash and physically turning up for lessons is no guarantee of learning. If it were, there'd be no need for final exams, would there? There'd be a simple form to fill in, with just one question: Have you attended 90% of the classes? If 'yes', congratulations you've passed.

No. Just because you're 'studying' doesn't logically imply you're learning.

So although there's a long list of resources you can get and activities you can do regarding your language acquisition, don't confuse them with making progress.

As well as progress, we also need to have the *feeling* of progress. We very well might be moving forward, but if we can't see it we get the feelings of frustration, futility and despondency, none of which are likely to get you bouncing out of bed early in the morning ready to do an extra hour's study.

The problem here is whereas some activities automatically give us a sense of progress, language learning doesn't.

32- Unless Jerry's chosen endeavour is to draw attention to himself so he can get mentioned in this book.

In order to establish if you are progressing, you need to be able to measure it. You can measure your kids' growth by marking their height against the wall, you can measure your progress at marathon running by counting the time it takes you to complete your practice circuit. But language is more nebulous, after all, how do you take two people and determine which of them can speak the best?

Trying to establish a language level is complicated. For a while, part of my job as an English teacher was to carry out level tests. I'd go into a company, interview a few dozen of their employees, and then have to assign them an English language level. Sometimes you'd have someone who could talk lucidly but had a limited vocab and an accent so thick it was almost opaque. Others had great pronunciation but took an eternity to string a sentence together. Others had mastered expletives but were barely able to conjugate the verb 'to be'. Others were able to read entire novels but struggled to produce a single spoken sentence.

So how can you measure yourself progressing with a new language?

The way I recommend is to use revision cards.

Revision Cards

If you need concrete and indisputable proof of your language learning progress, then I can wholeheartedly recommend revision cards. Not only do they serve as an ideal way of measuring your new language, they're an excellent way to learn.

I admit they are by no means perfect. They can't measure your pronunciation progress. They can't measure your verbal fluency or accuracy. But they do identify very well your ability to understand and, more importantly, recall new language. Realistically, it's the best option you have.

There are two types of revision cards: real and virtual. Use the ones you prefer.

When I say 'real', I'm referring to the 9.5cm by 6.5cm pieces of plain card you can get in packs of a hundred.

I like these real revision cards. They're easy to use, simple and flexible. A well-used, dog-eared set of revision cards can become like a close friend. I still have my old revision cards from my university days, ferreted away somewhere in the attic. No doubt the elastic band has shrivelled up and the colour-coded cards are a sadly faded shade of their former selves. But considering how much effort I invested in them and all the intimate time we spent together, I'm loathed to throw them away.

Nevertheless, I have to recognise this is now considered 'old-school' by some. The wood-pulp revision cards are being pushed out by the new kids on the block—the flashcard apps.

At the time of writing, AnkiApp was the bee's knees in flashcard apps. But history shows that today's bee´s knees have a habit of soon becoming tomorrow´s old hats as someone comes up with something even better. I started to use AnkiApp in parallel with my physical ones. It works very well. My flashcard app is one of the most useful tools I've found for making the most of all my spare minutes throughout the day.

There are lots of flashcard apps available. Many of them are free and they have several important advantages.

First and foremost, they're always at hand. As long as you always have your smartphone, you'll always have immediate access to all your revision cards. You never know when you're going to find yourself with a few minutes to spare. So a flashcard app means you're always prepared.

In some ways they're also more versatile. In addition to text, you can easily cut and paste images, video (GIFs) and even audio recordings. So, as far as your cards are concerned, your imagination is the limit, or at least what you can find, copy and paste from the internet.

Thirdly, the good flashcard apps use a 'spaced repetition system' (SRS). This means you automatically spend more time on the words you don't know and less on those you've already learnt and feel comfortable with.

Finally, flashcard apps don't spill out all over the floor, blow away or occupy a large bulk in your pocket. And if you back up your app on the cloud, even if your dog chews up your phone, you'll still be able to retrieve all your hard work without problem.

Although it wasn't available when I wrote these words, I'm sure it's not long before someone comes up with a way of being able to add new flashcards to their app more efficiently. I can imagine, when reading a text on your smartphone in your target language and coming across a new word, being able to click on it and, in addition to the usual 'copy' or 'look up' options, it will also give you the option of transferring it directly to your flashcard app, immediately creating a new revision card for that particular word or expression. Wouldn't that be marvellous?

Revision cards are really great. Here are my recommendations for using them.

1. Whenever possible, avoid writing your own language. If you write any text on the front, try to stick to vocab from your target language. This might seem impossible if you're starting from zero. But the sooner you stop translating and start thinking in your target language, the faster you'll learn. So write in your target language on both sides of the card. This might require a little bit of creativity on your behalf but the extra effort will be worth it. If your target language level is so basic it's just not possible then using badly drawn pictures involving stick-people, arrows and things that look like potatoes with legs is an acceptable alternative. Or if you're using a virtual system, copy and paste an appropriate image (or GIF) on the front.

2. Revise by placing the cards so the language you want to learn (or check you've learnt) is facing down. This requires you to recall the answer instead of just recognising it. It's good to understand a word when you see it, but it's much more useful to be able to mentally retrieve it whenever you need.

3. When you go through your cards to revise, first say the answer out loud, then if possible write it down and only then by finally checking your answer by turning the card over. It's very tempting to turn over the card and try to convince yourself you knew what was on the other side all along. Don't. It's a trap. The only way to prove you truly knew the answer is to have it written down before you look at the other side of the card.

4. Number the cards. This helps make sure you have all of them accounted for and is a way to see the 'age' of each card (the older ones being the lower numbers). Once you've got into triple digits, it's very satisfying to go through your whole deck and prove to yourself you've learnt your first hundred cards.[33]

5. Remember, never write just one piece of vocabulary on a card. Write vocab in context, preferably in short sentences or expressions that you're likely to use or encounter. This is really important.

6. Once in a while, it's worth going through your newly created revision cards with your language exchange partner or some other native speaker. It can be surprising the difference between what you understand to be correct with what theirs is.

7. If you're using real cards, try to carry them around with you at all times. Or, at least carry your latest revision cards around with you for regular revision throughout the day. Revising with your cards is an excellent way to pass those spare minutes while you're waiting for the kettle to boil, the film to start or the paediatrician to arrive.

8. Once a week, set time aside to go through all your cards, or at least the ones you're not absolutely 100% sure of. Sit down somewhere quiet with your deck and a pen and paper and don't get up till you've done the lot.

If you could get into the habit of making at least three revision cards a day, that's a minimum of ninety words a month (that's if you had just one new word on each card—which of course, you won't). Given you should be learning in chunks, most of your cards ought to have multiple new vocab which means you'll easily be covering more than a hundred new words and expressions each month. And that is just to start with. Once you get going you'll find the basic words you've learnt form a foundation. Building your vocabulary gets quicker so your active and passive vocab acquisition increases by up to ten words a day.

33- This is one of the few disadvantages of the flashcard app. There's no equivalent way of spreading them all out on the table and then, starting with the ones you fancy most, going through the whole lot.

Being able to see you've just increased your word-power by another hundred cards is a great feeling. And if you can count the number of new ones you've learned, you can plot them on a graph.

Progress Plotter

When I write, I have a clear objective (most of the time) of the word count I'm aiming for. For example, the target figure of this book, when I started, was about 35,000 words. I give myself a target date (or to be more precise, my publisher gives me a target date) and then I draw up a graph which visually represents this information. This graph I call my Progress Plotter and it's another wonderful perseverance tool I recommend to everyone.

Your Progress Plotter is a way of visually representing your progress.

You make a Progress Plotter like this: Draw up a simple graph (see fig. 2). At the bottom left is your starting date with no cards. At the top right is your objective: the finishing date with your final card count. In the example (fig. 2) my target is to learn 300 cards in three months.[34] You then join the starting point to the finishing point with a straight line (I like to draw this line in red).

This unassuming straight line is a powerful tool for helping you persevere with your project. It's extremely useful. If you put your finger on a date, slide it upwards until it gets to the diagonal line and then slide it across until you get to the left-hand axis, this tells you how many cards you should have learnt by that date to be on target. In short, this diagonal straight line represents the theoretical number of cards learnt. It's your line of intended progress.

Now for the practical part. On the same graph, you also plot your current achievement every once in a while (I recommend once a week) and join the points up as you go. This somewhat wobblier line shows your real progress. So long as it is above the straight line of intended progress you can be a happy bunny knowing you're on track.

34- With chunking, this would correspond to approximately 750 words.

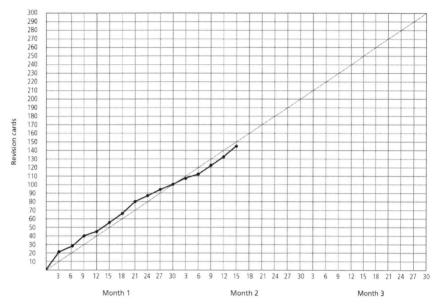

Fig 2. Progress Plotter

Counting revision cards works for measuring your own progress but at some point you'll be asked how well you speak your target language. If you reply by stating the number of revision cards you've learnt, you're just going to confuse them. Most people want to know how you speak a language in terms of everyone else's, not in terms of your revision card collection. This is why it's worth taking the occasional level test.

Level Tests

If you're not starting from zero, and by this I mean if you've studied in the past, or have been exposed in some way such as having family members who speak it, or have spent significant time hanging around your target-language speakers, then you should think about doing a level test.

At the beginning of my Catalan learning period I did two level tests: one online and the other by going to a language school who happily does them for free.

The difference was noteworthy. The on-line test was just a 'Pick the right answer: A, B, C or D', whereas the test that involved being face to face with a human being (called David in this case) involved listening and speaking. My level for the online automatic assessment was given as 'intermediate', a whole level higher than the 'elementary' I was assigned by the human. For most of us who've had almost no speaking and listening practice, this is no surprise.

If you already have some capacity to communicate in your target language, it's worth getting yourself level tested because sometime in the near future you might want to think about enrolling for an exam.

Enrolling for an Exam

The best way to measure your target language progress is by taking an exam in it.

If you sign up for a language course at night school or a language academy, then sitting the corresponding exam is easy. Your enrolment is carried out by someone else. But if you're going it alone or taking private classes then sitting an exam is not so straightforward.

The first thing to do is to find out what exams are out there and which level is the most appropriate for you.

Then you have to find out how to register for the exam which, depending on the organising body, can be months before the date of the actual exam.

I felt doing an exam in my target language would help motivate me. Having that specific goal with a date attached to it would give me something concrete to aim for. So after I'd recuperated from my level test, I decided to enrol myself for the exam by internet. But it wasn't as straightforward as I'd expected.

I looked up the complexities of enrolling in the exams, organised by the '*Generalitat*' or the Catalan local government, and the narrow window for entering yourself for the exams (which are held once a year in June) is February. February turned out to be a rather busy month for me, so it wasn't until the 22nd I finally got round to filling in the online enrolment form.

After a few clicks I found myself on the appropriate page. It said, 'Enrolment now closed'. Confused, I made a few more clicks. Was this the right page? Was this referring to the exam I wanted? I ended up with the same message: 'Enrolment now closed'. I found another page that said, 'Enrolment for the Catalan exams for 2017 will be from 2nd to 21st Feb'. I checked my calendar hoping that somehow the date would miraculously change but it still suggested today was Monday the 22nd of February. Bother!

Then I got a flash of hope. It was only nine o'clock in the morning. Maybe if I phoned them up there'd be some way for me to rush into the centre of town and enrol in person as they were doing the final processing. I dialled the number and I eventually got through to the enrolment department. What sounded like a friendly little old lady answered.

"Hello, I'm an incompetent fuckwit who's got the dates wrong for enrolling for the Catalan exam in June. Is there any way I could possibly make a last-minute dash to your centre to enrol myself now, please?"

"No" was the reply. She did add that she was sorry but the enrolment period was closed.

"But surely there's a way you could include just one late entry? It's not even 12 hours after the deadline"

"No."

I tried to point out that it meant more money for the local government coffers but, of course, in reality I was talking to a civil servant who I know for a fact are specifically recruited for their firm belief that bureaucracy and red tape are far more important than actually helping people.

"Would it help if I claimed to be a member of the royal family?" Apparently not.

One of the things I've learned about the Spanish system is the importance of asking the right questions. You cannot expect government employees to be helpful. All they're interested in is getting rid of you as soon as possible. So I asked, "Is there any way I can get to take an official Catalan exam this year?"

This threw her for a moment, there was a hesitation in her reply.

"Are you living in Barcelona?" she asked.

"Er... Yes," I replied, uncertain that this would be the best answer.

"In that case, no. If you were from outside Catalonia, you could sit the exams organised by the Ramon Llull Institute. Their enrolment is in March. I'm sorry."

I thanked her for her help and relaxed slightly. A new window of opportunity had opened up, one just big enough for me to climb through.

After another phone call to the Ramon Llull Institute, it was made perfectly clear I didn't need to live outside Catalonia, I just needed to physically *be* outside Catalonia to take one of their exams which are held worldwide towards the end of May, two weeks earlier than the one I'd been hoping to sit. The furthest exam was in Tokyo, but the closest one was in Zaragoza, just a three-hour drive away. It was beginning to look like a plan.

So it was three months later I found myself one Saturday morning in Zaragoza, with four other fellow candidates, each of us sitting at a small desk in a large and echoey room which looked like it might be used in the evenings for secret Freemason meetings. The walls were decorated with portraits of old men trying to appear important and demure. The floor was a time-worn ceramic that looked like it'd been regularly polished for many decades. On my desk were six sheets of paper, stapled together. This was my Catalan exam.

The Exam

If you've never sat a foreign language exam, it's worth knowing that almost all of them are divided up into at least five parts: listening comprehension, reading comprehension, writing, speaking and a grammar/vocab section.

The listening and reading parts can be divided into different tasks such as listening/reading for gist (e.g. Does Mrs. Muggins agree with her husband?) or listening/reading for specific information (e.g. How much does Mrs. Muggins finally agree to spend?).

The writing is usually some sort of letter written to a friend (e.g. to invite them to visit), potential employer (e.g. to apply for a job) or an organisation (e.g. to complain about their service).

The speaking part[35] can be an interview with your examiner or a controlled conversation with a fellow candidate. Be prepared to have riveting conversations about organising a party, deciding what to do at the weekend, asking for help or describing your ideal life-partner.

The grammar/vocab section can be comprised of multiple-choice, fill-in-the-gap or complete-the-sentence questions.

To do all of this can take over three hours. Remember to take a pen or two and make sure you go to the loo before you start.

If you're not sure how to go about enrolling for an exam in your target language you can find a list of language proficiency tests at

https://en.wikipedia.org/wiki/List_of_language_proficiency_tests

For example, if you're interested in learning Turkish, you have three exams to choose from:

- Turkish Proficiency Exam *(Türkçe Yeterlik Sınavı)*
- UTS - Distance Turkish Test *(Uzaktan Türkçe Sınavı)*
- TELC - The European Language Certificates

Once you've found out what exam options you have, you can then go about looking them up on the internet and finding out how to enrol. Mine consisted of filling out a short online application and paying the exam fee (about £30).

One final thing about exams: Get hold of some past exam papers. They really help. You might be able to download them from your examiner's website or, if you're lucky enough, you can find entire publications dedicated to giving exam practise. By going through a few of these, you can familiarise yourself with the structure. This is a good idea as it helps

---

35- I know it's childish, but I can't use the expression 'Oral Test' without smirking.

calm you down a little on the big day. Going through an exam paper with your language exchange partner can be a very productive way of spending a session.

When I looked at enrolling for my Catalan exam it was the first time I'd done an exam in 24 years. I was far more nervous about it than I expected. But, as I realised, it was just fear of the unknown. I decided to look at it as an adventure; after all, what was the worst that could happen? I figured the worst thing that could happen would be to suffer a gruelling three hours and fail miserably. But even that would be a learning experience. But best try and avoid it, no? So from the moment I clicked the 'Confirm enrolment' button in March, I felt a sort of tingle, a sudden exuberating urge to get to grips with this new language and prove to the world I could do it. This was real progress.[36]

Milestones

Your language learning journey will feel unbearably long at times. To keep the sense of progress it's useful to set Milestones. You can think of Milestones as smaller Goals you will make along the way to your main Goal.

Round numbers of revision cards learnt (20, 50, 100, 200) can serve as intermediate Milestones as can intermediary exams if you get the opportunity to take them. But you can set yourself as many Milestones as your creativity can come up with.

Consider the following:

• Your first book read

• Your first revision card learnt

• Your first film watched

• Your first Skype

• Your first time pronouncing a difficult word correctly

36- Six months later, on the 22nd of September I finally got my result. I passed!

- Your first i rregular verb dominated

- Your first month of studying

- Your first phone conversation

- Your first language exchange

- Your first private lesson

- Your first text/email/letter

- Your first song learnt

- Your first level passed on your language learning app

- Your first conversation with a native speaker

- Your first poem learnt

- Your first Study-Buddy session

- Your first exercise book completed

- Your first visit to the region/country

- Your first joke learnt

- Your first story told

- Your first native-speaker friend

- Your first time in a native shop/bar/restaurant

- Your first experience with the native-speaking police

I'm sure you get the idea. You don't have to settle for just the first. Your third month of study, your tenth level on Duolingo or your fiftieth revision card are also perfectly valid.

You can mark off important Milestones on your Progress Plotter (50, 100, 150, etc.). It gives you something to aim for in the medium term and helps keep your mind off that big goal at the end of that red line.

Your Goal Diary Revisited

As you continue your language learning journey, you'll pass many Milestones.

One of the functions of your Goal Diary is for noting all these down. Keep a record of your steps forward, all your small improvements, all your milestones passed (both the intentional ones and the unintentional ones). Make a note of any special discoveries or favourite words or expressions. Set down how you feel about each of these things and what you're looking forward to next.

One of the reasons why you should do this is because, once in a while, it'll do you good to go through your diary. Remembering all these positive experiences will help draw attention to the progress you've made since you started. It's not an objective way of measuring progress. But it is a way of stirring up your emotions.

My Progress Plotter was over a twenty-week period and so fitted on one sheet of A4. But I used this same technique to lose weight over six months. In this case I had a Progress Plotter for every month (as I was weighing myself every day). I found it rewarding to print off a miniaturised copy of each monthly sheet and stick it into my weight-losing Goal Diary. Looking back over the months to see how my wiggly line kept going down (most of the time) was a great boost to my morale when I was feeling predictably sorry for myself.

If you can become emotionally involved in your language learning, your Goal Diary will help buoy you up and push you along. You will start to feel good about your new language. It is very useful to be able to employ our feelings to help us persevere with our projects. After you've answered the following questions, we'll be looking at what I call Passion next.

Questions

- Why is measuring your progress useful?

- What are the advantages and disadvantages of revision cards?

- What does the diagonal straight line represent on a Progress Plotter?

- Why is it useful?

- Where could you get level tested?

- When and where would your nearest exam be held?

- What milestones would be the most effective to set for yourself?

- Have you got yourself a Goal Diary yet?

- Is there any way you could improve the way you use a sense of progress in your language learning process to improve your motivation?

Passion

"Once something is a passion, the motivation is there."

– Michael Schumacher, German racing driver

A Flickering Flame

Some people have natural drive. They have something within themselves—a burning ambition, a constant itch, a never-ending need to forge ahead. They are passionate about what they do. They might not always be successful but despite hardships and setbacks, they push on. Or to be more exact, they are pushed on by their incessant passion.

If you feel the same way about learning your chosen language, then good for you. Congratulations! You don't have to worry about motivation. You have plenty of it already; you are destined to succeed.

But if you are in the same boat as the rest of us, it's not so much an incessant passion you have burning inside of you, it's more like a tiny flickering flame of interest that could be easily extinguished at any moment.

As a language learner, one of your tasks is to try to kindle this flame, to coax it into growing stronger. The bigger the flame of passion, the stronger your motivation, which means the more effort you're going to put in and the more progress you're going to make.

Professional athletes understand this completely. Even though they're already keen and motivated, they also understand they could be even more keen and motivated. This is one of the reasons why professional coaches are so much in demand. Coaches fan the flames of passion not by appealing to the head of their athlete (e.g. by explaining the advantages of training harder) but by appealing to their heart—by inspiring, threatening or even insulting them to try harder. The coach only needs to find out what emotional buttons need to be pushed to get their client fired up. Once those buttons have been identified, all that remains is to push them as many times as it takes to get the job done.

If you want to optimise your language learning, you have two options. Fork out a small fortune for someone to stand over you 24/7 verbally harassing you until you get the job done, or to figure out for yourself just what those buttons are and try to push them as hard as you can yourself.

Your Goal Diary Revisited Again

Another reason why your Goal Diary is useful is it's an excellent way to push a few buttons and start kindling those flames. If you want to get the most out of it, you'll have already noted down what your reasons are for wanting to learn your target language. If you've made that list, go back and look at them now. If you haven't, take a moment to go back to chapter 3 and look at some of the reasons why you might want to learn your language.

Now look at each of your reasons you've identified. Consider them carefully. Think of what will be different once you've achieved your goal. Imagine what your life would be like. How would it be better? Allow that image to sink in. Feel those positive feelings start to flow through your body. That's a button being pushed. Do this for each of the reasons you've chosen. Push, push, push.

In addition to your Goal Diary, there are many other ways of generating drive. In the previous chapters, we've considered using simple Prizes which can generate small but important quantities of motivation. We've also considered how Progress can fan the flames and how an apparent lack of Progress can be a total passion killer.

Take these into account when stoking your fire.

But there's more.

Inspiration

When I started researching the different ideas and opinions about language learning, I looked at the videos of interviews and presentations given by some of the most successful polyglots of our time. Characters the likes of Benny Lewis, The Youlden Brothers and Tim Doner.

Benny Lewis is the charismatic Irishman who can speak seven languages and has his own website: *Fluent in 3 Months*.

Matthew and Michael Youlden are ginger-bearded Mancunian identical twins. If there's anything to do with languages, they're not far away. Their website is http://www.superpolyglotbros.com

Tim Doner is (at the time of writing) a twenty-year-old polyglot blogger having already learnt twenty-three languages.

I listened to all of them and many more. They are all intensely passionate about what they do. They talk about their successes and challenges with obvious enthusiasm. What's nice is this positive energy is contagious. It pours out of the screen and over you. As it does so, your mind starts to soak it up. It's as though your body absorbs the passion for languages simply by being exposed to these people. You might not understand how they've achieved what they've achieved. You might not follow everything they say. But after absorbing their passion, your motivation for languages can reach a new level. After spending just one day watching video after video I felt like going out and studying every language I could find.[37]

37- I have to add that this feeling only lasts a short while. After just a few days, I'd settled down again and was quite happy to stick with my modest single-language quest. Nevertheless, it's fair to say my motivation for it had been solidly strengthened.

If you haven't seen any inspirational videos yet, here are a few to get you going.

- Benny Lewis: Hacking language learning

- Chris Lonsdale: How to learn any language in six months

- Claudio Santori & Muezz Vestin: Secret to hack a country and learn language for free

- Dr Conor Quinn: Hacking language learning

- Gaston Dorren: Grow up, learn another language

- John McWhorter: 4 reasons to learn a new language

- John Sloan: Learn language emotionally

- Matthew Youlden: How to learn any language easily

- Scott Young & Vat Jaiswal: One simple method to learn any language

- Sid Efromvich: 5 techniques to speak any language

- Tim Doner: Breaking the language barrier

What If It's Still Not Working?

They say if the mountain won't come to Muhammad, then Muhammad must go to the mountain. If you're struggling to become passionate about your chosen language then maybe you should try combining it with something you already feel passionate about, or if not 'passionate', at least something you quite like.

What do you do in your free time? What do you do for pleasure?

If you love music, reading or poetry or if you're a Trivial Pursuit enthusiast,[38] then you have plenty of material for turning your target language practice into something fun and enjoyable. If your spare time is spent on car maintenance, cake decorating or wood-turning there are plenty of ways to turn a hobby into another tool for language learning. Learn the vocabulary relevant to your craft, hobby or pastime. Label your

---

38- At the time of writing, editions of TP had been made in 17 different languages.

tools, bottles or drawers in your target language. If you like gardening, do a search for gardening forums or Window Box Garden websites in your target language. If you love watching football, pick your favourite club from your target language country and start following them. Find a channel that broadcasts their matches with local commentary and become a faithful fan.

One of my 'passions' is public speaking. Not everybody's cup of tea, I grant you. But I understand I'm one of the few people who gets a kick out of standing up in front of a crowd and talking. I found it a very good motivator when I combined it with my language learning and made it one of my goals to give a ten-minute presentation in my new language to the Catalan public speaking group here in Barcelona. Once having made the pledge to give the talk, I was totally dedicated to learning how to give it in my new language while making as few mistakes as possible. Practising it wasn't a chore; it was a necessity. I found myself practising at every opportunity during those final few weeks before the big day.

The Big Day

The big day turned out to be a Tuesday evening in July. I eventually got to the venue just in time, hot and sweaty after having mixed up addresses which didn't help my state of nerves at all. My audience was to be the Catalan public speaking Club 'Som-hi'. I'd been kindly invited to speak there by Gemma, the president of the club.

'Som'hi' meet in a lecture room on the fourth floor of a private secondary school in the middle of Barcelona accessed by one of the slowest moving lifts in the city. I finally made it to the room where about fifteen people were chatting to each other. Almost all of them were complete strangers to me, which didn't help calm me down at all. I did recognise Gemma who briefly welcomed me as everyone started to take their seats.

Fortunately, there were a couple of speakers ahead of me. I've no recollection of what they talked about. Not because I didn't understand their Catalan, but because I was concentrating on my speech, repeating bits of it over and over again. I could feel my nervous energy rising by the minute. I started to doubt whether this had been such a great idea.

I was just starting to check on the nearest escape exit when the inevitable happened: the speaker before me finished, someone said my name and I found myself standing up and slowly walking to the front of the audience. I hoped I didn't look too nervous. I took a moment to breathe. I looked at my audience in a way that would hopefully fool them into thinking I was perfectly confident and under control. I opened my mouth and began giving my very first public presentation in my target language.

Ten minutes later, it was over. I got a very welcome round of applause from my new friends. I loved them all! I felt more relieved and more elated than I have in a long time. It had all been worth it. I was on cloud nine. All my practice had paid off. It couldn't have gone better. I'd managed to remember all of my presentation, without stumbling or hesitation.

It had worked. My passion for public speaking had helped me focus on learning my target language. Without having put myself through this, I just wouldn't have put in the same effort. My motivation would not have been the same.

Now, I'm not for a second proposing you do a public presentation, too. I'm simply demonstrating how combining your target language with something you enjoy can increase your drive.

Television

It's estimated the average adult watches more than three hours of telly every day. In some cases, a lot more.[39] You can now get TV programmes broadcast from almost anywhere in the world. Some of it's free, some of it you're expected to pay for. But if you're an avid telly addict, how much practice would you be getting if you watched 30 minutes every evening?

If you're thinking of giving it a go, here are a few points to bear in mind.

The first is to make sure you understand what you're letting yourself in for. If you're just starting out, you're going to understand diddly squat.

39- An in-depth survey from 2015 found the average adult in the U.K. spends a daily 3½ hours watching the telly, while the Spanish, French, Germans and Italians watch slightly more. All of us Europeans are beaten hands down by our cousins on the opposite side of the Atlantic, who watch 4½ hours of television every day.

You'll be faced with strange foreign celebrities gabbling on twenty to the dozen and you won't get a word of what they're going on about. Not only that, but you'll start to feel there's some sort of conspiracy where everyone on foreign TV has agreed to talk twice as fast as normal in order to put you off trying to learn their language.

There is no conspiracy. This is absolutely normal. But don't be put off. Your new-language mental-processing system isn't even in first gear yet, whereas all those you see on the small screen are effortlessly cruising in sixth. You will catch up with them one day, but for the moment you need patience. Patience and lots of practice.

Your first objective for watching your target language TV is to get used to the pronunciation and feel of the language. It's important to understand you're not expected to understand anything at all.

The next step is to start listening for any patterns, any expressions that stand out. Anything that's repeated frequently is probably useful. Spend time learning them.

Do a bit of channel surfing until you find something that looks like a homemade soap opera. Then stick with it. Local series are great for language learning as they involve real conversational language in context and they show something of the culture of the language, too. They're much better than imported, badly-dubbed soaps. I simply couldn't bring myself to watch *East Enders* in Catalan. It's just WRONG in so many ways. I even watched a few episodes of *Fawlty Towers* in Catalan which was completely bizarre.[40] It might work for the Catalans but it doesn't work for me. So my recommendation is to stick to home-grown produce.

Once you've identified the name of your TV series, you can start making some serious progress. Look it up on the web and find out the names of the characters, who they are and what they're about. If you're very lucky, you might even find a description of the next episode.[41]

40- Especially as in the Catalan dubbed version they make Manuel out to be from Mexico.

41- You know, the sort that says, "In episode 165, Juan explains to Gertrude, he needs money for a sex change, while Omar discovers his secretary, Jasmin has a secret love-child living in the attic. Meanwhile Fritz has just successfully tested his homemade incendiary device and is about to make sure Fernanda's housewarming party is one the Fratelli family will remember for a very long time."

Half the battle is maintaining your concentration. It's all too easy to get to the credits to discover you've spent the last twenty minutes thinking of something else. One way to do this is to always watch with a pen and paper. Keep jotting stuff down to check out later (don't worry about the spelling; there'll be plenty of time to correct it later, too). Write down the stuff that's repeated frequently or expressions that sound familiar. If you've gone for ten minutes without making any notes, it's a sure sign you've stopped concentrating.

Take breaks. Concentrating on a foreign language TV series is much, much more demanding than watching one in English. If your programme is thirty minutes, take a break halfway through. Have a cup of tea, walk about, go outside, stick your head in a bucket of cold water. When you come back, go through your notes, look up anything you need and identify the three or four top expressions worth transferring onto your revision cards. Then do the same for the second half.

Don't try to be too ambitious and overdo it. If you have half a dozen new chunks of language after each time you watch, that's plenty. More than ten and I'd say you're trying too hard. Less than four and you've not been paying attention.

If you have the time, watch the episode again. It's good for consolidating your new chosen vocabulary and you'll be surprised to notice stuff you missed the first time.

Video

Just like TV series, films also offer a great way to experience your target language. Anne taught herself French partly by watching French-made films. She started off with Amélie[42] and worked her way through as many as she could get hold of.

Apart from having better production qualities, better acting and better music, films also have a couple of other differences. One useful one is you

---

42- Or to be more precise, *Le fabuleux destin d'Amélie Poulain* (The Fabulous Destiny of Amélie Poulain) is a beautifully gentle comedy written and directed by Jean-Pierre Jeunet and has a wonderfully haunting soundtrack by Yann Tiersen.

can pause them while you're writing down any noteworthy language. This is great for you but can be annoying to the rest of the family. Another advantage is most films come with subtitles, usually in the language they were made as well as English and a few more thrown in for fun.

It's tempting to have the subtitles on while watching. Try to resist if you can. Certainly don't put the subtitles on in English. If you do, you'll simply watch the film while reading them. There's part of your brain which is devoted to processing incoming language. If you're giving it input in English, it can't focus on the spoken dialogue which is exactly what you're supposed to be doing. It just isn't possible to read a book and listen to conversation at the same time.[43]

Furthermore, subtitles can be notoriously unreliable. Writers have to make sure the subtitles keep up with the dialogue. Given most of us can process the spoken word faster than the written word, the result is dialogue in subtitles tends to get filtered or simplified. This is great if you're trying to follow the gist of what's going on, but not so good if you're trying to understand details of what you're hearing.

Also, should you ever be tempted to watch one of your favourite films dubbed into your target language, the fidelity between audio and subtitles can be even worse. I'm convinced the people responsible for dubbing and the people responsible for translating subtitles work in different buildings or different sides of the planet. I've seen films dubbed where the some of the subtitles are very different to the dubbing. It's as if the script had been translated by two separate people. I suspect it's something to do with trying to get the dialogue to fit the movements of the actors' mouths while trying to get the subtitles to stay short and sweet. Whatever the reasons, if you're going to practise your target language, you're much better off watching material from that country than watching *Star Wars*, *Titanic* or *The Wizard of Oz* dubbed.

43- If you're in the living-room enjoying a thoroughly good read while someone, possibly someone you're married to, starts talking to you from the kitchen, you have zero chance of mentally taking any of the conversation on board—a fact I keep pointing out every time the wife tries to tell me what to add to the shopping list.

Recommendations for watching stuff in your target language:

- Watch programmes made in your target language.

- Research the plot before you watch if possible.

- Don't watch with English subtitles.

- Be wary of subtitles in your target language.

- Don't try to understand everything.

- Focus on useful expressions, common language and stuff you recognise.

- Use the pause button and write stuff down.

- Take regular breaks.

- Watch multiple times and try watching without any subtitles.

Film and television are two examples of where you could do something that's enjoyable that involves your new language. But whether it's weaving, surfing or yoga, if you can find a way of incorporating your studies, if you can find a way of dovetailing your old hobby and your new language together, your chances of progress will get better.

There is one thing most of us get passionate about which we haven't considered yet: people. It's very useful to consider how our motivation is affected by others. Whether friends, family or famous celebrities, they all influence our behaviour. Why not answer the following questions before we move on to the next chapter about Peer Pressure?

Questions

- How have strong emotions influenced your (in)ability to carry out long-term projects?

- What are your strongest positive and negative emotions regarding your reasons for learning a language?

- How can you make the most of these?

- What are your sources of inspiration?

- What language learning activities do you enjoy the most/least?

- How can you make more of these?

- What other activities/hobbies do you enjoy? How can you combine them with learning your target language?

Peer Pressure

"The key is to keep company only with people who uplift you, whose presence calls forth your best."

– Epictetus, Greek philosopher

The Christmas Party

Many years ago at a Christmas party, Malc, an old friend of the family, had just got his first mobile phone. But he was a bit of a worrier as well as bit of a scrooge. He was suspicious of this new-fangled technology and was worried he might end up talking to someone in Caracas or somewhere which would cost him a fortune for a wrong number. So he decided to make his premier call by phoning my cousin Josie[44] who was also at the party. Assuring him he was being silly, my cousin ushered him into the next room and told him to call her from there. In the meantime, she handed

---

44- To be absolutely accurate, my cousin Josie was actually called 'José' but her parents thought that was how posh people spelt Josie.

her phone to me and asked me to answer in Spanish. It's impossible to convey Malc's reaction and the subsequent ridicule on paper, but I assure you, it was worth learning Spanish just for that!

Languages are all about experiencing social interactions. Some are fun, some are deadly serious.

The joke we played at the Christmas party made me feel acknowledged. My efforts to learn Spanish had been publicly validated by my family. It was a highly motivating experience. It was like being awarded some social badge of recognition.

We are all social animals. By this I don't mean we all like to go out and party every night. No. What I mean by social animals is that we are all genetically wired to be sensitive to 'others'. These 'others' can be real or imaginary, close family or complete strangers, a huge crowd or a single individual. But whoever they are, we are attuned to feel their presence and value their opinion of us—or at least what we think is their opinion of us—and we almost always modify our behaviour to take it into account.

Consider your situation right now. If you were exactly where you are now but completely alone with zero chance of being disturbed, would your behaviour be the same as it is at the moment? Or conversely, if you are completely alone right now, would your behaviour change if you knew that someone else was observing you? I understand some people suffer from this sensation of feeling constantly observed, that an invisible entity is watching them all the time and it makes their life very stressful.

An old colleague of mine insisted on drawing the curtains when she was at home, even during the daytime, because of the feeling that people were watching her. Who these people were and why they had nothing better to do than to lurk about in the bushes for hours in her front garden I have no idea, and she found it difficult to justify her reasoning. Nevertheless, she closed the curtains.

But for the rest of us, this natural tendency to modify our behaviour due to how we are perceived or pressurised can be a blessing if used in the right way. How we are socially influenced by people doesn't just happen; we can shape it to our advantage. We can intentionally cultivate positive

Peer Pressure which will beneficially influence our chosen behaviour. There are plenty of ways to achieve this.

They all involve other people with whom you share a common interest— either speaking your target language, studying it or even just any form of self-improvement. If someone perceives you as having a common interest, they will welcome you with open arms.

We've already met Brenda (Case Study 1) who lives in a little English-speaking corner of the southern coast of Spain. She used the Peer Pressure of a group of friends to learn Spanish and, after eight months, passed her first Spanish exam. But there are plenty of other sources besides.

Language Exchange Groups

A language exchange is where a mixed group of people get together in order to get some practice speaking different languages. When I first came to Barcelona, I was fortunate enough to live within a two minutes' walk from a successful language exchange group in the city centre—successful because it was regularly attended by dozens of keen people all eager to practise and let practise speaking a new language. There was a comfortable balance between natives wanting to learn a foreign language (mostly English) and expats wanting to learn the local languages. Furthermore, the group met in the spacious back room of a bar and the background music was kept to a minimum. This meant there was an interesting mixture of faces every week, enough physical and acoustic space for the attendees to interact and a convenient supply of alcohol to help jolly things along. I was a regular there for many months practising my Spanish. It helped me a lot.

Twenty-five years later and forever optimistic, I thought it would be a good idea to find a language exchange for my Catalan. With the usual trepidation one experiences when going along to meet a group of completely unknown people for the first time, I set off one dark January evening in search of useful language practice.

It was a mixed experience. Unlike the group from years before, this one met in a noisy bar which appeared to have been chosen for its appalling acoustic properties, which made hearing anyone not sitting immediately next to you almost impossible.

When the session started there were seven of us sat at a large circular table all looking a bit sheepish and reluctant to open our mouths for the obvious reasons. Then this fellow in his early thirties ambivalently ambles across, sits down and grunts a hello to us. I was optimistically hoping for a warm welcome for having travelled across the city, forgoing my comfy, warm and above all quiet home to support his cause and hearing how lovely it was to have an internationally renowned writer turn up to one of his sessions. I would have settled to be asked my name and be introduced to the rest of the attendees. What we all got was a wall of indifference; a lack of interest that was astonishing considering he was apparently the instigator of the evening's proceeding.

Finally, he went away which allowed us to get back to the idea of practising speaking and without the organisational skills of Captain Indifference, we managed much better.

I was fortunate enough to be sitting next to a pleasant and patient lady from Mallorca. She explained to me she was there to improve her written Catalan. I thought she might have come to the wrong group. Though I was pleased she had because she kindly asked me a selection of user-friendly questions and gently waited until I could organise my brain around the answers. After about an hour of mixing and matching, most people had had enough. Each made their excuses "Oh, is that the time? I'm afraid I need to get going" but in Catalan of course.

And that was that. I'd successfully survived my first Catalan language exchange.

I thoroughly recommend investigating these groups. If you can find one in your area, give it a try. They're a fun way of getting real speaking practice and you get to meet new and interesting people, too. They can be a great source of useful contacts and psychological support, all of which can help you persevere with your plan.

But if there is no language exchange group in your area, don't give up just yet. It might just be the sign for you to set up your own.

Set Up Your Own Group

Setting up a group is like blowing up a balloon: it's the first bit that's difficult. Once you get some momentum going it gets much, much easier.

Find a place to meet. Preferably nice and quiet enough to easily hear conversation. Back rooms of pubs early evenings are good for this before the crowds arrive. Posh hotel lobbies are also excellent as the decor is more chic and the seating more comfy.

If possible, get a couple of friends to come along to give you support. For a newcomer there's nothing more embarrassing than turning up to a new group like this, only to find out you're the only one. If there are already a few of you, newcomers feel more relaxed.

Then advertise. Where would you look for a language exchange group? Notice boards of book shops? Community centres? The local library? There are some wonderful apps that are especially designed for helping people connect in groups. Check out Meetup. Nothing to do with dating, everything to do with finding out what's happening in your city regarding stuff you're interested in.

Spread the word. Tell everyone what you're doing. Slowly, if you keep at it for a few weeks, people will start to get the idea. You'll get a few regular attendees and once you gain momentum you'll find your group starts to effortlessly freewheel along.

One-to-One Language Exchanges

Although I've had many happy memories of language groups, nowadays I much prefer one-to-one exchanges. It's not as hit-and-miss as a group. With one-to-one you know who's going to be there, at least in theory, and you're guaranteed to get the language practice you want.

If you go for this option, you have two alternatives: meeting face to face or by videoconference. As I was fortunate enough to be living in an area where there are lots of people who speak my target language, I first chose face-to-face. All I needed was to find someone who wanted to practise their English with me and had a compatible timetable.

Asking around, I discovered one of the neighbours, Raul, was interested in practising his English. 'Great', I thought. We arranged to meet the following Tuesday afternoon while the wife went to pick the kids up from school. It was a short walk down the hill to his house at the prearranged time but, as A.A. Milne would have said, the more I rang on his doorbell, the more he wasn't in. At that moment my phone rang. Hey presto, it was Raul.

"I'm sorry but I've had to collect my daughter from school. Can we leave it till next week?"

"No problem," I replied partly annoyed, partly relieved.

I walked home back up the hill determined next time to text him before the meeting to make sure it was still on.

After our shaky start, my sessions with Raul were fine. We always met at his place and he's very hospitable providing coffee and biscuits to help jolly the conversation along. As we live in the same neighbourhood and both have young children, we were never stuck for conversation.

But with one-to-ones, this is not always the case. When one (or both) of you has a limited command of the language, conversation can be difficult. Never underestimate your mental incapacity to fail to come up with something to say. The effort of struggling with a new language can be quite paralysing. You can soon achieve the cerebral dexterity of a potato. To stop this from happening, I suggest following a few simple guidelines.

- Prepare: Have a subject to focus on. Take along a photo, a book or an interesting item you found in the attic.

- Have an objective: What, linguistically speaking, is the point of the session? Do you want to practise speaking about the past? Or practise vocabulary to describe people? Do you want to go through your revision cards to make sure they're correct?

- Establish conditions: The norm is to linguistically share the session 50/50. That way it's balanced. Another option is to alternate languages with each meeting: one day in English, the next day in your target language. But I find it's too easy to say 'I'm tired, today. Let's talk in my language.' By linguistically sharing the session, you're guaranteeing you'll get the practice whether you feel like it or not.

- Corrections: It's annoying to be corrected every half sentence. It's much better to note down any important corrections for your partner to go over when appropriate.

- Set a timer: If you're going to have a successful meeting, it's quite likely you'll lose track of the time. So if your session is one hour, set a timer for 30 minutes so you know when to change languages (most likely, you have a timer on your phone).

- Make notes: You won't remember it afterwards. Write down the things you're corrected on. Write down the new vocab you come across and, if necessary, make notes for your partner. It's always useful to go over them during those last few minutes of wrap-up time.

- Post production: Straight after the session, write up your notes, identify the most important bits you want to learn and make flashcards. If you leave it too long, you'll find yourself a few days later struggling to read your own notes trying to remember what on earth 'grlmbk' was supposed to mean.

Don't expect your first language exchange partner to be your ideal match. It's a bit like dating: Deep down we might all be the same, but I'm convinced that on the surface at least a quarter of us are barking mad. Some people are far too intense to make good exchange partners, others are too laissez faire, giving the impression that they don't care what you say—right or wrong. If it's not working, politely move on.

I was very fortunate. At the height of my studies, I had three language exchange partners. In addition to Raul, I found two of the parents of kids who are in the same class as mine were also interested in improving their English. Thus, the bar next to the local primary school became a regular spot for our language exchange sessions, both in the morning after dropping the kids off as well as in the afternoon before picking them up.

If you don't have native speakers conveniently living in your area, don't despair, there are plenty of opportunities to get one-to-one language exchanges over the internet.

Check out the following sites, they're all free:

http://www.babelyou.com

http://www.babelvillage.com

http://www.conversationexchange.com

http://www.easylanguageexchange.com

http://www.italki.com

http://www.languageforexchange.com

http://www.speaky.com

But bear in mind, an exchange partner is just a normal person who happens to speak your target language. They are under no obligation to commit or put you under pressure to commit. They are unlikely to be experts who know what is best for you. Furthermore, they won't be setting you homework or correcting your study methods. And of course, while half your time is spent practising your target language, the other half isn't. Which might not be satisfactory for you, either.

If you want commitment—if you want your sessions to be as optimally productive as possible—you should consider getting yourself a personal teacher or tutor.

Private Teachers and Tutors

If you have the financial flexibility, I recommend you get a one-to-one teacher.

Having your own private teacher means having someone who will guide, motivate, adapt and push you to bring out your best. They are experts and will tell you what to do and how to do it providing you pay them enough money. And there lies the problem, because given that money and time are related, the logistical problem of getting you and your private teacher to the same place at the same time can be very time consuming. This is why private classes over the internet have become so popular. If you haven't tried it yet, you should.

You can't spend much time looking at language learning before someone mentions italki.

italki is a website that helps language learners connect with online teachers and native-speaking language partners to get that all-important person-to-person communication experience.

It sounds like a great opportunity especially if you don't have anyone local who can teach you. It gets great reviews from Benny Lewis[45] and if it's good enough for Benny, it's good enough for me.

So I thought I'd give it a go. The first thing I did was to go to the App Store and download the italki app for free. Once in, you get to enter your chosen language, your native language and your time zone. You then scroll through all the teachers and tutors available to see who you want to try.

My first choice was a teacher called Helena who was based in London. She seemed like a great match, plenty of experience (thousands of hours) so obviously, I thought, she must do a good job. Then I saw she charges $35 an hour. Now call me a miser, but I know what the going rate for private language classes face to face in Barcelona is (about 20€/hour). $35 is close to double that. So I don't know how Helena does it but I'm afraid I'm not paying that much an hour. The next one on the list was Sandra living in Paris. Sounded rather romantic but, at $25/h, still out of my range.

I started to become somewhat disenchanted with italki. Even when I found Andreu who was only charging $16/h I started to think, 'Well, he must be rubbish if he's only charging that'. This was very uncharitable and illogical of me. At least I could have given the fellow a chance.

So I decided to check out a few more online tuition sites. That's when I discovered Classgap. I liked it. With Classgap, many tutors offer a 15-minute free get-to-know-you session, which was absolutely fine by me. I scheduled one with Jenni.

The following week, after a brief period trying to sort the microphone on my computer, I found myself talking to Jenni, 150 miles away. I was impressed how it worked. Jenni was adept at controlling the screen,

---

45- Polyglot and author of 'Fluent In 3 Months'

reducing her image to leave the rest of the screen to show texts, images and a space where we could both type stuff. She was great. I immediately booked a full one-hour session for the following week.

Jenni was everything I expected from a good teacher. She used praise, humour, encouragement, patience and of course a ton of positive Peer Pressure. I had eight classes with her over the two months leading up to my exam.

The positive Peer Pressure you can receive from languages groups, one-to-one exchanges or teachers/tutors can be very powerful. But I'd like to take the opportunity to remind you that having real meaningful conversations with these people is one of the most important actions you can do to learn your target language. I'm not making these recommendations just so you can get Peer Pressure. I'm recommending them because according to every single website, book and lecture by polyglot gurus, this is how it's done. Yes, there are other ways of getting Peer Pressure as we're about to see. But there's only one way of getting real meaningful language practice and that's by making the effort to find native speakers and speaking to them.

Of course, once you've started to do that you'll also be frequently asking them to help you improve your pronunciation, constantly making notes about your mistakes and also about the expressions you wanted to use but didn't know how to say. After, each session you need to take time to review your notes, select the most important language points from the session, make revision cards using chunks of language so you can revise them several times a day so, all being well, you don't make the same mistake twice. This, fundamentally, is how to learn a language.

Study Buddies

Getting back to other forms of positive Peer Pressure, a study buddy is someone you team up with who is learning the same thing you are.

The great thing about a study buddy is they are in exactly the same boat as you. They are the best person for comparing notes, sharing ideas, asking questions and talking to about what you're going through and how you feel about it because they are going through it, too.

My best study buddy ever and who also turned out to be my lifelong closest friend is Gary. We studied our A-levels together at sixth form (maths and physics) and spent hours and hours comparing notes, working through passed papers or asking for help when either of us were stuck. Gary was a shoulder to cry on when things were tough and a source of inspiration whenever we got together (after 35 years, he still is). In addition to the time studying together at school, we also spent many hours on the phone when one of us were struggling with our homework. We were lucky to have some great teachers, but if it hadn't been for the emotional support of my study buddy, I doubt I would have got the grades I did.

Having someone on your side who is trying to do the same thing as you can be a huge help both in practical terms (such as helping out when you get stuck) and also in terms of morale. A study buddy can give you encouragement when you're feeling frustrated or give you a kick up the arse when you're lagging behind. It can make all the difference to your perseverance.

Consider that Scott Young and Vat Jaiswal are a couple of amazing linguists. They learnt to be fluent in four languages in just one year. It sounds extreme because it is. The two of them decided to pack up and go to live first in Spain, then Brazil, then China and finally South Korea.

The fact they were able to achieve fluency so well is undoubtedly due to their rule of never speaking to each other in English—a technique which forced them to focus on their target language to maximum efficiency. But here my question is if they had each tried to do the same journey but alone, would they have been able to keep up the willpower to have followed it through for twelve months? Maybe they would, maybe they wouldn't. But what I'm absolutely sure of is without having each other as a study buddy it would have been much, much harder for them to keep going.

The only problem is study buddies aren't so easy to come by. It's difficult enough finding a good friend, let alone one who will willingly agree to start studying the language you want at the same time. This is where language exchange groups and forums can be useful. There you automatically have people who are interested in the same thing. You don't only have to practise talking in your target language; you can also talk to fellow learners about how they are coping, about what works for them, about any good resources they've discovered or any studying tips they'd be happy to share with you.

But if you don't have a group that you're part of, it doesn't mean you shouldn't try. All you need to do is ask around. In a similar way of setting up a language group, it's a question of spreading the word and letting people know you're looking for someone who's learning your target language (or is interested in starting) to provide a bit of moral and practical support.

If you can't find support from someone who's interested in studying your target language, you can always try to get support from someone who isn't. That's what Praise Donors are for.

Praise Donors

Having moral support, even if it's from someone who isn't doing the same thing as you, can also help keep you going.

I was very fortunate to have a father who understood this. He was keen on self-improvement, always trying his hand at new skills, whether musical, yoga, do-it-yourself or languages. He taught himself Swedish and German and when I moved to Barcelona he taught himself Spanish as well. He was a great listener. He'd pay attention to my explanations of my next crazy idea, ask a few poignant questions and then tell me to go for it, whether it was moving to a different country, setting up my own business or thinking about settling down and getting married. He was always interested in what I was doing and always had more than a few words of encouragement. It was always rewarding to talk to him. I miss him very much.

Praise is another type of reward for good behaviour. It's a form of positive recognition we looked at in chapter 6.6. It's a powerful motivator.

Talking to a Praise Donor is like taking your car to the petrol station and filling up with fuel. You might feel run down and demoralised. You might feel you're not getting any better and that you're never going to be able to speak the language. But just talking to your Praise Donor can be enough to recharge your batteries and get you going again.

If you haven't already got a Praise Donor, go out and get one. Ask. It's the squeaky mouse that gets the cheese, as they say, and you've got much more chance of getting recognition and praise if you tell your most trusted allies that's what you need to help you persevere towards your goal.

Pick the person you have most confidence in and let them know you'd like them to help you with learning your target language. You can calm them down by pointing out they don't need to speak a word of it themselves, but you will need to take up their time occasionally by talking to them about how your language progress is going. Just talking to them about what you've been going through recently and getting a bit of positive feedback can work wonders for your perseverance.

Making Your Objective Public

Never underestimate the power of Peer Pressure. We are programmed to be influenced by the behaviour and opinions of those around us. It comes in two forms: compliance and defiance. Compliance is where you want to appease someone, you want them to approve of you, to accept you, to value you. Defiance is where you want to prove yourself to be different, capable, rebellious, independent. Recognise these forces and learn to turn them to your advantage. If you keep your objectives to yourself then there'll be very little pressure from outside. But if you share your goal, the social pressure of meeting their expectations might be just what you need to make the mark.

When I openly declared, at the start of the year, that I would give a 10-minute speech in Catalan, I found the social pressure to be tremendous. It's quite possibly one of the most challenging things I've ever done. The nerves I suffered on those final few weeks, those final few days leading up to the moment. I was so nervous the day of my speech I couldn't eat. I felt my stomach had been taken out and put back in the wrong way round. But all of these nerves were really, really useful. They motivated me to knuckle down and double up my efforts to learn my target language. If I hadn't publicly declared the challenge, it would have been so much easier to back out—an option I was still genuinely considering in the final few days before. The Peer Pressure definitely helped.

Role Models

When I was a kid, I loved cartoon strips. I loved comics like *MAD* (and later *VIZ*) and cartoon strips like Shultz's *Peanuts*. But my favourite cartoonist was Johnny Hart who drew *The Wizard of Id* and *B.C.* I loved his work. For many, many years Johnny Hart was my hero, my role model. I didn't just love reading them, I loved drawing them, too. I studied Hart's style and copied his drawings. I dearly wanted to be a professional cartoonist.

After forty years, times have changed. Instead of a cartoonist, I'm now a writer and I love giving talks and seminars. My heroes have changed, likewise.[46] But even so, they still provide me with a sort of target, something to aim for, track and follow. They continue to inspire me. Showing how it's done. Showing it *can* be done. Motivating me to put in that little bit of extra effort one day at a time.

With respect to language learning, I don't have a specific role model but that doesn't mean you can't. There are plenty to choose from. I've mentioned a few characters already in the section on inspiration (chapter 8.3) such as Benny Lewis or the Youlden brothers. But whereas inspiration can be provided just by listening to a 15-minute talk or reading a book, Role Models are people who you closely identify with and admire. People who are doing stuff you'd love to do, too. Here are a few more for you to check out. You only need to find one you 'click' with to get that little bit of extra motivation you need.

John Fotheringham (http://www.l2mastery.com) is an author, curriculum designer, educator, entrepreneur, linguist, and nutritional therapy practitioner who's been learning and teaching languages for over two decades. His website focusses on Japanese.

46- If you'd like to know my role models I'd have to say Seth Godin, Sir Ken Robinson, Terry Pratchett, Douglas Adams, César Millán, Bill Bryson, Dave Allen (comedian), Steven Fry, Richard Curtis, Sir Richard Branson and my father, Llew Gibbs. If pushed further I'd add Han Solo, Aragorn son of Arathorn, Ron Weasley and James Bond.

Donovan Nagel (http://www.mezzoguild.com) is from Australia, has a degree in Applied Languages and has been travelling the world for over 14 years. He speaks French, Italian, Georgian, Turkish, Irish (Gaeilge), Korean and Russian. His site covers many more.

Simon Ager (http://www.omniglot.com) is a professional language blogger who lives in Bangor, North Wales, who speaks English, French, Welsh, Irish, Mandarin, German, Japanese, Scottish Gaelic, Spanish, Manx and Esperanto. If that's not enough, he also speaks a bit of Taiwanese, Cantonese, Italian, Portuguese, Czech, Russian, Breton, Dutch, British Sign Language (BSL), Cornish, Swedish and Toki Pona.[47]

Susanna Zaraysky (http://www.createyourworldbook.com) has studied eleven languages (English, Russian, French, Spanish, Italian, Portuguese, Serbo-Croatian, Ladino, Hebrew, Arabic, and Hungarian) and speaks eight of them. Born in the former USSR, Susanna has travelled to over 50 countries. Her goal is to empower people to use music and media to learn foreign languages.

Olly Richards (http://www.iwillteachyoualanguage.com) started learning languages when he was 19 years old and working in a cafe in London. He now speaks eight languages, including French, Italian, Spanish, Portuguese and Cantonese.

Kerstin Hammes (http://www.fluentlanguage.co.uk) loves learning languages. She's a native German speaker who speaks twenty-five languages on her YouTube video and runs her website to help you develop a healthy language habit.

Lindsay Dow (http://www.lindsaydoeslanguages.com), from England, does languages. Not in a Debbie Does Dallas kind of way. More in the sense that she learns, teaches, blogs, vlogs, eats, sleeps and breathes everything to do with languages.

47- Toki Pona is a minimalistic synthetic language designed by linguist Sonja Lang. It focusses on simple concepts and elements that are relatively universal among cultures. Lang designed Toki Pona to "express maximal meaning with minimal complexity". The language has 14 phonemes and approximately 120 root words. It is not meant as an international auxiliary language but is instead inspired by Taoist philosophy. Not a language for asking the whereabouts of the nearest toilet.

Steve Kaufmann (http://www.thelinguist.com) is the Canadian co-founder of LingQ, an online language learning system. He can speak sixteen languages and shares his passion and knowledge for language learning via his website.

Gabriel Wyner (http://www.fluent-forever.com) started learning German because he needed it for his job as an opera singer. Since then he's learnt French, Italian, Russian, Hungarian and Japanese.

But in the end, your language learning role-model doesn't have to be someone famous who is followed by millions. It can just be someone local you know whose achievements you admire. Even if they've only learnt one other language (or even if they're just starting themselves), it might be all the Peer Pressure you need.

Linguistic Liaisons

Let's get this straight. If you're in a steady relationship, this perseverance technique probably isn't for you. But if you're free and single, why not include a bit of flirting as part of your persevering arsenal? It was my French teacher who pointed out that "The best teachers are the ones with long hair" which I took to mean attractive young females who can have you mesmerised from the very first 'Bonjour'.

I'm definitely not suggesting you adopt a mercenary attitude and start using and abusing other people's emotions just to improve your language. But if you're on the lookout for a dating partner, why limit yourself to someone local when it's so easy to date online with someone who's just a short flight away?

Remember Charlie from Case Study 2? Charlie had to learn German for an unexpected job opportunity. The whole study process was an effort until he met Tania. While he was studying, Charlie decided to spend a week visiting Cologne. Tania was staying at the same hotel on business. They found themselves propping up the bar in the evenings like two solitary characters out of an American film. Charlie was looking for anyone to practise his German with and Tania was impressed with an Englishman whose German vocabulary was more than ten words. When he returned home, Charlie kept in touch with Tania via texting and FaceTime. From then on, learning German didn't seem to be such a chore any more.

However, it is extremely important to get one thing clear. If you are not looking for romance with your teacher/tutor/study buddy/exchange partner, if you feel there is any unwanted sexual tension, deal with it as soon as possible. Nip it in the bud straight away. Make it clear you're uncomfortable about the situation or simply stop the sessions before it becomes a major problem.

Coach, Mentor or Accountability Partner

Have you ever seen a film where the hero is in the gym doing some gruelling physical exercise and next to them, is someone shouting at them to push on and do more? That person is the hero's sports coach: someone who knows just what to say to get our hero to do what it takes to keep going, to push on further, longer, higher. The coach doesn't necessarily have to be an athlete as well. They could be an overweight slob with a megaphone. It doesn't matter. They just have to know the hero well enough and care enough to get them to put in the effort, to push through their natural barriers of resistance such as tiredness, lack of motivation and lack of confidence. The reason why top sports-stars have coaches to plead, cajole and insult them is because it works—not only for sports but for anything else. And that includes learning a language.

If we all benefit from having someone shouting us on from the side-lines to keep going, then isn't it a good idea to get one?

If you have the money, you can pay someone to do this. It's what coaches are for. But it's not that difficult to find someone who'd be able and willing to do it for free. A mentor is someone who has been there and done it already. They have a good idea about what you are facing and what motivational support you might need.

An accountability partner is simply someone to whom you can solemnly promise to do a certain amount of work by a certain time and who, in return, will make you feel awful if you don't keep your word. Wives, mothers and grannies, for example, are very good at this. Apparently they get lots of practice.

Talk to your friends and colleagues to see if anyone would be prepared to help. But make sure they are the right person for the job. Have they done this sort of thing before? Do they recognise and value your objective? Is there a conflict of interests? If your partner sees your language learning project as competition for your time, they might not be the best candidate. If your friend is uncomfortable about you trying to better yourself, avoid bringing up the subject. The people closest to you do not necessarily prove to be the best sources of motivation.

Consider the people you know. Who do you trust, respect or admire enough to value their opinion and follow their advice? It might be a family member. It might be your Head-of-Department or your neighbour or the bloke who works behind the bar. Anyone whose opinion you value will do. They don't even have to be alive.

Although Becky lives in London, her mum had been from Oslo. But Becky had no memories of her mother, just a photo on her dresser. Her English father, who didn't speak any Norwegian at all, had soon lost touch with his wife's small family. When she was a teenager, Becky decided to teach herself Norwegian. Her accountability partner was her mother. "There was no-one I knew who I could talk to. I didn't like the idea of chatting to complete strangers over the internet. So I began having conversations with things in the house. I know it sounds a bit silly but I talked to the clock, the fridge and the kettle. Then one day I was in my room and I talked to the photo of my mum. It happened then, I swear she smiled at me. That was when it began. I didn't talk about anything morose or sentimental. It was just normal stuff, thing's I'd done that day." Every night Becky would talk to the photo of her mum on her dresser, practising what she had learnt. As she says, it was a bit like writing a diary but speaking it instead. When she lacked motivation, she'd imagine what her mum would say to her and how proud she would be to hear her little daughter speak her mother tongue. That was what kept her persevering. Becky now speaks Norwegian fluently and has made contact with her uncle on the other side of the North Sea, all thanks to the social pressure of a mother she never knew.

Negative Peer Pressure

Beware of attitudes that go against your objective.

Peer Pressure is a powerful thing. It can spur us on to do the most amazing things but it can just as easily hold us back and stop us in our tracks.

Such phrases as "You're not still wasting your time with that Portuguese nonsense, are you?" or "I tried to learn Japanese for three years. A complete waste of time that was!" or "Learning Language is for linguists. I'd stick to something you're good at" are not meant to help you. They're meant to stop you, because you trying to improve yourself is making the other person feel uncomfortable. They might feel envious you're doing something they wanted to do but didn't. They might feel betrayed you are doing something that doesn't follow their approval. They might feel threatened by you learning to do something they don't feel capable of.

Whatever the reason is, it's not likely to motivate you onwards and upwards. It's more likely to make you doubt your actions and capabilities, especially if the person in question is someone whose opinion you'd normally value. You'll find yourself saying 'Maybe they're right', 'Maybe I am wasting my time', 'If [insert name here] couldn't do it then what chance have I got?'.

This sort of negativity is dangerous. It can easily turn into a self-fulfilling prophecy. If you start to believe you can't, then your destiny is almost sealed. You become demotivated, so you don't put in so much time and effort. This means you don't practise and revise so much, which in turn means your progress gets less and less until you find your 'valued opinion holder' smugly pointing out "See? I told you so!"

Don't let this happen to you.

Spot negative influences and try to avoid them. Or if you can't change the company, at least change the subject.

Search for the antidote to negative peer pressure. Find those worth-their-weight-in-gold Praise Donors who will give you a dose of positivity. It's another small but important part of your language learning puzzle.

To finish this section on Peer Pressure, let's look at another Case Study after answering the following questions.

Questions

- How much positive peer pressure are you receiving? Who from?

- How much negative peer pressure are you receiving? Who from?

- What can you do to improve this balance?

- How would you rate your usage of the following to help you learn your language?

  - ✓ Language exchange groups

  - ✓ One-to-one language exchange partners

  - ✓ Private teachers and tutors

  - ✓ Study buddies

  - ✓ Praise Donors

  - ✓ Role models

  - ✓ Linguistic liaisons

  - ✓ Coaches, mentors and accountability partners

- How could you get more positive peer pressure from each of these groups?

- Are there any other people who could help motivate you with your target language?

Case Study 3: Anne

Anne was twenty-three when her granny passed peacefully away. When it happened she felt the family was about to fall apart. Her grandmother had been the linchpin that kept the different parts of the family together: the English part and the French part.

Granny Flo was originally from Paris but had become the teenage bride to an English civil servant. They soon moved to Lincolnshire and had one son, Anne's father. But her granny had been the oldest of four daughters and had left behind a substantial extended family.

One of them (Aunty Fabi) would come to visit regularly bringing her three children Nathalie, Veronique and Thierry who were a bit older than Anne. But for some reason, Anne's father had never learnt to speak French, so it was always Granny Flo who translated when Aunty Fabi & Co's English was lacking. But slowly as the kids grew up, their visits became less and less frequent. On the day of the funeral, it was the first time Anne had seen her favourite cousins for over three years. That was when she decided if she wanted to keep her French connections she needed to do what her father had so fantastically failed at: learn French.

- She certainly had no lack of people to communicate with. She was able to connect with almost all of her cousins on Facebook. From there on it was mostly a case of Messenger and Google Translate.

- Anne's goal was to spend the following summer travelling round visiting all of her family across the Channel (like both her parents, she was an only child). She had just under a year to learn French well enough to be able to have a decent conversation.

- She realised it was regular practice that counted. So she kept a regular eye on her Facebook account and made regular comments and daily posts in French, to start with by using translation apps.

- She did lots and lots of chunking. She kept a list of all the useful expressions she came across. If her relatives were using the expressions, then that was good enough for her. She made a note of them and recycled them whenever she could.

- She made it clear to everyone she wanted to improve her French, spoken as well as written. She openly asked for support, advice, recommendations, anything that could help. She was delighted when Thierry suggested having regular language exchange sessions via Skype. He wanted to improve his English for his job.

- She had no end of recommended films, music and novels. She started reading for pleasure and discovered French authors such as Julia Deck, Katherine Pancol and Muriel Barbery.

Anne booked her summer flight in October. "That was the 'no turning back' moment," she says. "Once I had my flight booked, I knew I had no choice. I had to make it work. When I told everyone I was coming to visit, they were all 'Hooray! Anne is coming! We'll organise a party.' Any excuse to open a couple of bottles of *Chateaux Plonk* with that lot, I tell you!"

Questions

- What do you think were some of Anne's reasons for learning French?

- What were some of the learning techniques she used?

- How did Peer Pressure influence her?

- If you had been Anne, what might you have done differently?

- What else could you take away from Anne's experience?

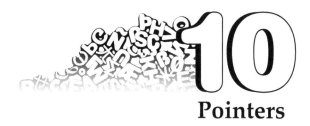

Pointers

"People need to be reminded more often than they need to be instructed."

–Samuel Johnson, Lexicographer

A Limited Resource

We've looked at how to reward ourselves with Prizes and the importance of having a sense of Progress. We've considered some ways to use Passion and Peer Pressure to increase our motivation.

Once harnessed, these four factors are powerful tools. Nevertheless, they all have one problem: They all require our focus.

We lead busy lives, now more than ever. If you're anything like me, you have things to do, people to see, deadlines to meet, places to go, decisions to make, issues to deal with, birthdays to remember, social media to check out and home-entertainment to enjoy. Let's face it: your attention is a limited resource much in demand.

Even with the best intentions, at some point you're going to get distracted from your daily language learning activities. After all, each one is so small it hardly matters if you skip one occasionally, does it?

Of course it matters. Each time you skip one of your small daily activities, you're adding a little bit more grease on that slippery slope to failure.

"Just this once won't hurt" is one of the most common excuses for giving up. You forget you've been saying "Just this once" for a week. What's worse is after just a few days you even stop saying 'Just this once' at all. You simply stop bothering. Suddenly, voilà!, you've gone a whole month without sticking to your plans and your goal starts drifting off out of reach.

There are two ways of dealing with this situation: the external and internal. The internal we'll be looking at in the next chapter. The external is the way we can organise our environment to help guide us along so we carry out the actions when we ought to.

I'm a big fan of Moonpig. If you've never heard of them, Moonpig is an online greetings card company. In the old days when it was someone's birthday, I'd catch the bus into town (in those days 'town' was the centre of Sheffield) and go to a shop that had millions of greetings cards row after row after row. I'd spend half an hour trying to decide which one was the most suitable and then get the bus back. After writing out the card with the most profound and sincerest greeting I could muster, I'd then pop it in the envelope, lick it, seal it and then take it up the road to the post office to get a stamp put on it and sent. The whole process must have taken most of the morning. Moonpig saves this time by offering the same service by internet. You peruse the offer of cards on their website, select one, write out your greeting and press the send button. Your card is then printed and whisked off to the birthday celebrator without you even having to put your coat on. The whole process takes less than ten minutes. But the important point here is, the following year, Moonpig emails you a reminder seven days in advance that you might be wanting their services again soon. It increases business for them and it saves you from that 'I'm-sorry-I-forgot-your-birthday' experience.

When our attention is in constant demand, these reminders are important to redirect our attention and to guide us to do something we weren't thinking about the moment before.

Our world is full of things that guide our behaviour: alarm clocks, traffic lights and stand-on-the-right signs. A dirty pile of dishes serves to remind us they need cleaning and the note you left yesterday on your keyboard reminds you today to send information to Steve. They all exist for one purpose: to point our behaviour in the right direction when we're thinking about something else. For this reason, I call them Pointers.

Pointers can be very effective. So long as we notice the pointer, our corresponding behaviour happens almost automatically. Our alarm-clock goes off and we get up. The green light turns to red and we put on the brakes. We don't put any effort into making a decision whether to comply or not, it just happens. Our reaction is automatic.

This is why part of my bedtime routine is to set out my work for the following morning so when I get up, it's all there, ready to start the day. A colleague of mine sets out his jogging clothes next to the bed at night. When he gets up, they serve as a pointer to what to do next.

Programme it

One simple way to point our behaviour in the right direction at the right moment is to programme it. If you have a smartphone, you have an agenda.

If you set in your agenda a time and date for an activity, the likelihood of you doing it is much higher than if you left it to some vague time in the future. If you're going to spend five minutes each morning reading the news (in your target language, of course) or going through your revision cards, then put it in your agenda.

Your Skype sessions, your language exchange meetings, your bedtime reading—all the things that are going to help you learn—programme them. Make them happen.

You probably think this sounds obvious. Yes, it is. But if you looked at your agenda right now, how many of your language learning activities have you actually got programmed for the next few days? Even though spending just a few minutes here or there reading, listening or revising is 'trivial', it all counts and is so easy to forget if we don't remind ourselves.

Whatever you choose to do, if you put it in your agenda you're more likely to do it.

Other Reminders

When you leave that little note on your keyboard to send a document to Steve, it doesn't matter if you see it at 8am, 2pm or a week next Tuesday. It's not the time, it's the place that counts. You'll see the note the next time you sit at your computer. That's when you'll send it.

We now have wonderful apps on our phones that let us send ourselves reminders depending on our change of location. Amazing!

The wife has her own method of reminding herself to do stuff. She draws a cross on the back of her hand and then, six hours later, asks me why she has a cross drawn on the back of her hand to which I reply I haven't the foggiest. She then wanders off to triumphantly return a few minutes later with the answer. Not the most infallible of methods but she insists on doing it.

I much prefer the old-fashioned and more reliable way of reminding myself to do something by leaving stuff in the most obvious of places. If it's important for me to read a few pages of my target language bedtime reading, then I leave it on my pillow. If your breakfast routine is to watch an episode of your favourite TV series in your target language, then set up the DVD before you go to bed and leave the remote on the breakfast table.

If the reminder is unavoidable and the next step to carrying out your desired action is easy, you'll find yourself doing it almost automatically.

The Default Option

Even better than setting up your video the night before is to have your target-language film kept permanently in the player. This means whenever you're feeling a bit lethargic and can't be bothered to get up and choose something to watch, hey presto!, your video-viewing has already been decided.

Program your internet browser so the first page that appears is automatically one of your favourite target language sites. If your car still has a CD player, make sure before you turn the engine off, you replace whatever you've been listening to with a CD of your target language music or audio book.

I used to be practically addicted to the news. I had the BBC News App on the home screen. So every time I switched on my phone, I saw the little red icon which was just begging to be pressed. The result was I spent far too much time looking at the news and not enough on more important things like revising.[48] Since discovering the error of my ways, I now have my favourite language learning apps (Notes, AnkiApp, Google Translate and Duolingo) on my home screen and have relegated BBC News to the next page.

What are the most useful applications you have on your computer for language learning? Set your device to automatically open them up each time you turn it on. Put them onto your desktop or home screen for optimum effect.

Programme your screensaver to come up with some interesting expression in your target language instead of its current default setting.

Impress your friends and confuse your enemies by setting the language of all your electronic devices to your target language.

Keep a small notebook and pen in the pocket of all your coats or bags, that way you'll always have something where you can jot down those useful expressions you discover during the day.

48- or writing, or washing the dishes, or spending quality time with my family, or doing my income-tax returns, or walking the dog, etc., etc., etc....

Keep your best language books or reading material in full view and within easy reach, either on the coffee table, the dinner table or your bedside table. If you put them away, out of sight or out of reach, your tired future-self will be too distracted to remember they're there.

Whatever you do, take the thought process out of the equation. Your future self is going to be too busy, too distracted, too forgetful to remember. Anything you can do to make your target language the default option will increase the probability you'll do it.

Post-its

I'm not a great fan of post-its. I tried them. I honestly did. But I simply never got into them. But I do know people who swear by them, almost converting Post-its into a sort of new religion: 'Post-itism'—the fervent belief that the key to eternal happiness depends on small pieces of coloured sticky paper.

If you're thinking of giving them a try, I'd recommend a few basic rules.

- If you're sharing your space with other people, let them know what you're doing and get their agreement/support if possible.

- Write three or four words per Post-it. More makes it difficult to take in at a glance. Less and you're not chunking properly.

- Make the effort to actively remember. Cover the Post-it up with your hand and try to recall what it says before you have time to read it.

- Take them down before they fall down. It's easy to develop Post-it blindness: the inability to notice Post-its that have been there for over a month. Give each one an expiry date (write it in the corner in small lettering) and take them down accordingly. You can choose your own timeframe but honestly, if you've had *'te peihana huka'* stuck to the sugar bowl for six months and still haven't learnt it, there's no helping you.[49] Try origami.

49- *'te peihana huka'* is Maori for 'sugar bowl'

One tip I do recommend involves Post-its and the TV If your telly is anything like mine, you've got hundreds of stations to choose from and a few of them just might be in your target language. To save yourself channel surfing, put the channel numbers of these stations on a Post-it and stick it next to the screen. That way, when you collapse on the sofa at the end of the day, you won't need to absentmindedly flick through the channels; you'll know exactly what channels to go to.

Tomorrow's To-do List Today

One of my favourite pointers is my 'Tomorrow's To-do List'.[50]

I'm not a big fan of to-do lists. In fact, I think to-do lists can be counterproductive. If I wrote out a list of everything in my life I have to do, I'd be faced with a huge list of stuff that would put me off ever doing it simply due to its size.

But what works for me is to take five minutes at the end of the day to consider my three main language learning objectives for the next day. By now, I hope you realise tomorrow you'll have lots of little objectives throughout the whole day. So here I'm talking about the most significant three. They could be to go over a past exam paper with your exchange partner, to order a new book, to download some new music or to learn and practise a couple of new expressions you've just discovered. I find three is just the right number—not too many, not too few. If it's appropriate, I programme them into my agenda; if not, I keep my 3-point list as a note on my phone. At the end of the day, one of my prizes is to go through my little list and satisfyingly cross each one off knowing it's been a productive day.

Charts and Graphs

Throughout this book, there are persevering tools such as the Star Chart or the Progress Plotter. These are sheets of paper you stick on the wall

---

50- To be truthful, as I prepare this list for my tomorrow-self, it's called 'Today's To-do List' so when I see it tomorrow, tomorrow will be today. You get what I mean, don't you?

and fill in as you go. These, too, serve as Pointers. Their very existence reminds you that you have something to do today. If you kept your Chart or Plotter in a folder somewhere hidden in a desk drawer you're likely to forget about it. You'll know it's there but your attention will be drawn elsewhere. By sticking these sheets somewhere highly visible such as your bedroom, kitchen or office wall, you're far more likely to pay attention to them and regularly fill them in.

These charts were of great help to me. I ended up using two: The Progress Plotter and the Habit Farm (see next chapter). It was nice to carry out my little end of the month ritual of taking the completed ones down and replacing them. It was another example of that satisfying feeling of progress. I printed off the new one, carefully removed the old one without pulling too much paint off the wall and then sellotaped its replacement back in position.

Before throwing them away, I take a photo of the sheet, print it out in miniature and stick it into my Goal Diary. It's another way to boost morale when I look back to see how things have improved.

When/Thens

There are situations you simply can't programme into your diary and neither can you leave yourself a reminder or Post-it because they happen in unpredictable places. You're in a meeting or bar and discover the person you've just met speaks your target language. How do you react? What do you say?

If you're calm, relaxed and sober, the answer to what to say and how to react might be obvious. But when our mental capacity is limited by tiredness, stress or alcohol, the obvious reaction is not always so obvious. This is where When/Thens help.

A When/Then is a prepared automatic reaction you set yourself. It's a bit like sticking a Post-it on the inside of your head. Such an example could be 'When I meet someone who speaks my target language, I will say "You're from [insert place here]? That's great. I'm studying [insert language here]. I've been studying it for [insert duration here]."'—but in your target language, of course.

If you're a higher level you could try 'When I meet someone who speaks my target language then I'll speak to them in it' or 'When I'm at a social event, then I will make the effort to find out if anyone there speaks my target language.'

When I'm out in Barcelona, almost everyone speaks my target language of Catalan but because I don't look like a native, waiters, shop assistants and friendly local police all initiate conversation with me in Spanish. My Spanish is fine, but it's Catalan I want to practise. Yet it's so easy to simply go with the flow. It takes effort to change the language once a conversation has started. So one of my When/Thens is 'When someone starts talking to me in Spanish, then I'll say "I'm studying Catalan, do you mind speaking to me in Catalan so I can practise?"' which most people are only too happy to do.

Here are a few more:

- When I come across a useful new word or expression then I'm going to write it down.

- When I go to the loo, then I'll do ten revision cards (one session on AnkiApp).

- When I'm on the bus/metro/train, then I'll listen to a podcast in my target language.

- When I'm about to finish a language exchange, then I'll go over my notes with my partner to make sure I've got things right.

- When I'm reading in my target language for pleasure, then I'll always underline the new/useful vocab I want to learn.

- When I go to the doctor's/dentist's/hairdresser's/tax office, then while I'm waiting I'll read, revise or talk to someone in Catalan instead of aimlessly leafing through the same crappy out-of-date magazines they still have from the last time.

As I said, Pointers are external ways of dealing with our lack of focus. They are things we set up to remind ourselves.[51] After you've ruminated over the following questions, we'll have a look at the internal ones

Questions

- When was the last time you were so distracted you forgot to do something important?

- What Pointer could you have used to remember it?

- Do you currently use any Pointers to help guide and remind you to study?

- What new Pointers could you use?

- How many of tomorrow's important learning activities have you programmed?

- Do you have any default options set up?

- Could a simple tool like a Star Chart, Progress Plotter or Habit Farm (see next chapter) help focus your attention?

- What internal Pointers (When/Thens) could help you improve your learning?

- What Pointers can you set up now to help guide and remind your future self?

- Would it be worth experimenting with a few different ideas to see what works?

51- I know When/Thens are not exactly external, but they're still things we have to set up and so I've included them in this chapter.

Periodic Actions, Habits and Routines

"You don't learn a language, you get used to it."

– Khatzumoto, founder of http://www.alljapaneseallthetime.com

Just Like It Says on The Tin

As we've just seen in the previous chapter, a pointer is something that reminds you what to do the moment you need to do it. You see (or hear) it and you react. But if you do this enough times, you'll get to a point where you no longer need the pointer. Your activity will become automatic. It becomes part of the way you are. It becomes part of your habitual behaviour, the stuff you naturally do without giving it hardly any thought at all.

There are three types of behaviour which fall into this category: periodic actions, habits and routines.

Periodic actions, just like it says on the tin, are things we do regularly at predictable times such as going to work, taking your medicine and celebrating your birthday. You never question them. You do them automatically.

Habits are things you do in a certain way. The way you chew your food. The way you pace about when you're nervous. The way you sneeze. You don't think about it, you just do it.

Routines are sequences of behaviours—lots of different actions we are used to carrying out one after the other. The process of cleaning our teeth, making a drink or going to the loo are all things we do the same way, time after time after time.

Some periodic actions are routines, such as getting up for work. Some routines are habit, like the way you handle your keys from when you arrive at your front door to collapsing on the sofa. But all of them are carried out with hardly any thought at all.

If we can convert our language learning into periodic actions, habits and routines, we can start to learn automatically rather than having to make a decision each time the opportunity knocks.

One example of a periodic action is attending language classes.

Language Schools

If you need to improve your foreign language skills, enrolling yourself on a course at a language school is the first option for many. There are language schools in most major cities. People like language schools. They work, don't they?

Let's consider the reasons why.

Firstly, as we've all been through the educational system, the concept of learning something by going to a building where 'learning' takes place is a comfortably familiar one.

When you sign up, you have a clear goal (or contract) to achieve X level by attending Y classes which will take Z amount of time.

You are given a timetable. This you put onto your calendar which serves as a pointer, reminding you that next Wednesday evening is your next language class.

When you sign up for a course and get the course material, you immediately get a sense of Progress.[52] Later, you'll see yourself 'progressing' through the course by the crosses on the calendar and the passing of each chapter in the course book.

When you attend your first class, you meet your fellow classmates. You start to feel a connection with them as you clearly have at least one thing in common. The social aspect of language learning is one of the top reasons why some students attend. You start by getting to know each other. You form social connections. You give mutual support. You provide peer pressure. You start to feel obliged to attend class because you are one of the group—a group where you are accepted and welcome.

If you stop attending, the money you paid will be lost and you'll also lose your social status as a regular and reliable member within the group. You risk being seen as letting them down, as being a failure. All of these factors serve as potential Punishments hanging over your head that help motivate you to continue attending.

Eventually, your attendance becomes so regular that Wednesday night becomes language learning night. At that point you have it cracked. Your behaviour—specifically, preparing and making the journey to your place of study—becomes automatic. No longer do you need rewards or punishments, nor do you need peer pressure or reminders. Your behaviour becomes so ingrained that once your course is over, the hole it leaves in your life feels so big, it's uncomfortable not to be attending classes. You feel 'strange', a bit ill at ease and so the thought of signing up as soon as possible, especially when you find out your old classmates have signed up already, gives you some reassurance that after the holidays your life will be returning to normality. This is the power of habit.

The only problem is learning a language in a class is amazingly inefficient. Our educational system shows this. Children can study French at school

---

52. Even though you haven't learnt anything except maybe the name of the school's secretary.

for an hour a week for six years and yet still fail to have a basic command over the language. Whereas if a child attends a bilingual school, where half of their classes are in the second language, where they use it every day, that child can finish the academic year being able to converse in the second language quite comfortably.

A language is not an academic subject like maths or history. It's a skill like swimming or riding a bike. You don't learn it by attending a class once a week; you learn it by applying it as often as you can every single day.

If you are set on attending your local language learning institution, that's absolutely fine. But if you use the techniques in this book, it's worth checking if your contract allows you to switch classes and move up to the next level because you're going to find yourself racing ahead of everyone else.

So what are the periodic actions, habits and routines that are the most useful for learning your target language?

The answer is entirely up to you. It's not so much a question of what, it's a question of how many and how often.

My regular activities included:

- Reading children's stories

- Going through my revision cards

- Listening to the radio

- Repeating useful phrases out loud.

- Talking to someone

- Trapping new language by writing it down

- Making new revision cards

- Writing out a 'tomorrow's to-do list'

- Keeping track of my progress

- Keeping my Goal Diary up to date

Yours might be completely different. It doesn't matter.

If you are about to start learning a language, you can consider all the different studying methods there are. You can select the ones that you think are going to work best for you. You can toy with the different ideas of how to fit them into your day. You can plan and pontificate as much as you like. But in the end, it's not about what you're going to do in the future; it's about what you are doing now.

What are you doing now, today, to practise and develop your target-language ability? So long as you're doing something, that's great. Yes, there is a hierarchy of activities. Yes, some activities need time to plan. Yes, some tasks are more effective than others. But if you haven't done any of them by the time you go to bed, you're not putting into effect the Sorites Principle: the constant application of insignificant actions when coherently focussed will inevitably lead to dramatically significant results.

In a nutshell: Anything is better than nothing.

So go back to chapter 4: Pick out a handful of your favourite activities and start doing them today. If you like, another habit you can cultivate at the end of the day is to look back and ask yourself 'What have I done today to improve?'

But if there is one activity which stands out as being the best habit to develop, all language learning gurus point in the same direction: practise speaking the language from day one.

Talk To People

In the café nearest my kids' school one of the barmen is called George. He almost always has a smile on his face. He's pleased to see his customers. He warmly greets each one and provides excellent customer service. George isn't from Barcelona, he's from Nigeria and his mother tongue is Igbo. Now, I've already got my hands full trying to learn Catalan, so I'm not interested in learning another language at the moment. But I was curious nevertheless. So I asked George how to say 'thank you' in his language. '*Dalu*' was the reply. So now, every time he serves me, I reply with '*dalu*'.

After just a few days, the word became instinctive and George's smile gets bigger every time he hears me speaking his language—even if it's just one word.

The habit to cultivate here is to speak in your target language with anyone you can. Whether it's the barperson, a colleague at work or a neighbour. If you can get into the habit of speaking to them in your target language every time you see them, it will help consolidate your fluency. I'm not talking about discussing anything complicated. Simply saying the equivalent to 'Good morning, isn't it a lovely day?' or 'Hello, how are you doing?' is fine. Don't worry about the reply being incomprehensible, once you start, the person will realise your language level and respond accordingly. This habit serves three purposes: it gets you used to initiating a conversation in your target language; it helps ingrain the functional language into your long-term memory; and it helps you overcome embarrassment by realising the world isn't going to end when you don't understand a reply. Once you've developed the habit you can start to build on it by increasing the length of the conversation.

Talk to Yourself

They say the only way to be guaranteed a decent conversation is to talk to yourself. This doesn't necessarily hold when you do it in an unfamiliar language. But if there is no one available to practise talking to at the moment, it's your next best option.

As the skill of speaking is more important than the skill of reading and writing, it's only logical to get as much speaking practice as possible. The problem with this is your language partner isn't always conveniently around when you feel like a bit of conversation practice. So the next best option is to do a Shirley Valentine and talk to the wall or the dog or, in a more down-to-earth approach, talk to yourself.

It worked for me... eventually.

I initially found the conversation to be too repetitive to have any sort of real value. I inevitably kept to the vocabulary I was already familiar with.

So rather than conversation, I started to practise the latest useful chunks, 'conjugation explanations' or revise whatever it was I'd been learning that day. If you can, speak out loud. It's good for pronunciation practice, too.

But even with this I found myself going over the stuff I already knew rather than the stuff I really needed to practise. I was getting into a rut.

There were a few tricks I discovered which helped solve this. One of them was to pick a vocabulary area (such as food, body parts or things you can do with a paperclip) and start to name as many items as you can come up with. This forces you to mentally stretch. Then, with each item you come up with, you put that word into a sentence, trying to make each sentence as different as possible.

Once you've extended your language a bit further, another trick is to tell yourself a well-known story such as Cinderella or The Three Little Pigs. The advantage of doing this is it forces you to rummage around in the bottom drawer of your memory in search of the vocabulary you thought you knew but don't have readily at hand in order to tell the story. This immediately stops you from simply repeating the easy vocab. It also forces you to be creative with the vocab you've learnt so far. This is an important skill in itself. When you come to a word you don't know how to say, such as 'a glass slipper', try to work your way around it (a shoe of same material as window?) or at worst, have a guess (*eon krystal klog*?) and move on. Don't be worried about making mistakes. Your focus should be on fluency rather than accuracy.

One of the nice things about telling a story is it gets you to look at linking words such as 'but', 'then', 'because' and 'suddenly'. These words are important as they show how one sentence is connected to another. They're not the sort of vocab you normally focus on. Telling yourself a story is a great way for drawing your attention to what you need and what you don't know yet.

Another tip. Don't feel your story has to be told using the past tenses. I know the traditional beginning to all stories is 'Once upon a time there was/were/lived, etc.'. But if you're not au fait with the past tense it can lead to all sorts of problems. Keep your story in the present tense to start with. Beginning with a simple 'There is/are…' is absolutely fine. No-one will ever know. Your secret is safe with me.

But when you have got to grips with the past, perfect and future tenses, another trick to practise is to explain what you did yesterday, so far today or what you're going to do later on. This again forces you to use vocabulary outside of your comfort zone, which is what learning a language is all about.

Remember: it's important to have these conversations out loud. You need to practise pronunciation, too. You're training your mouth as well as your brain. The good news is it's never been easier to do this. Before, if people saw you talking to yourself they just thought you were mad (or conspiring with the devil and have you burned at the stake). Nowadays, if you do it sat in your car or while wearing headphones, people just assume you're on the phone.

So far in this section, we've covered what your regular language-leaning activities should be. Now let's look at a few ways to turn your chosen activity into a habit.

Routine Surgery

Routines are a series of actions we carry out regularly. We can take advantage of our routines by cutting them open and grafting on an 'alien' activity which we want to cultivate. The new activity essentially becomes part of our old routine.

For example, if five days a week you have lunch in the office canteen, you could develop the habit of saying to yourself the name of each food item in your new language as you load it onto your tray. You could take a minute to go through your latest revision cards as you're waiting in line. Once the new habit has been successfully grafted onto the old routine, every time you carry the old one out, the new one will be repeated, too.

Most of us have at least four solid routines: getting up, going to work, returning home and going to bed. If you can incorporate one small learning activity into each of these, you'll be carrying out 20 learning actions a week while making hardly any effort at all.

Two guidelines: Just because you've consciously decided to include a new activity in your chosen routine, it doesn't mean it'll take root overnight. Just like a skin graft, it needs time to take root. You need to support your new activity via the means we've already covered: Prizes, Progress, Passion, Peer Pressure and Pointers. Especially Pointers, which are well suited to this sort of action. So if you decide to go through your revision cards each morning before you get out of bed, prop them up against your alarm clock so you'll see them or put them inside one of your slippers.

The other guideline is your new activity should be short and simple. If you try to include learning six irregular verbs or writing a three-page essay, it's not going to stick. It's too much effort to ever be done without much thought.

One of my commuting habits was to listen to the radio. I had it permanently tuned in to the appropriate station (a current affairs station: no music, just reporting and interviews) and while I was driving I repeated out loud any useful phrase or expression I recognised. My bedtime routine included going through revision cards, reading at least one page of my target-language storybook and planning out my 'tomorrow's to-do list'. None of these I considered particularly difficult. Nevertheless, over time their effects make a difference.

But maybe you're the sort of person who considers cultivating just one or two small habits to be insufficient. In that case, you might be interested in something a little more challenging.

Weekly Timetable

We considered earlier how you can programme an action into your agenda. This serves as a useful pointer for when you need to do it. If this action is worthwhile, it's a good idea to make a habit out of it and do it regularly along with all the others you're doing, too.

This means converting your agenda into a timetable.

Your agenda app will already give you the option of making a programmed activity into a regular event. But it's simply not enough to put your regular language learning activities into your agenda. You need something more.

Get a paper and pencil (or start honing up your spreadsheet skills) and draw yourself up a weekly language learning timetable.

I found a weekly timetable to be the best, just like the one you had at school. It's big enough to put in the number of small details you need but small enough to mentally cope with.

Language Learning Timetable

	Mon	Tue	Wed	Thu	Fri	Sat	Sun
6:00							
7:00	Flashcards	Flashcards	Flashcards	Flashcards	Flashcards		
8:00							
9:00	Radio	Radio	Radio	Radio		Flashcards	Flashcards
10:00					Lang exchange		
11:00		Class			Radio		
12:00							
13:00							
14:00	Flashcards	Flashcards	Flashcards	Flashcards	Flashcards	Flashcards	Flashcards
15:00		TV Series		TV Series			
16:00		Lang exchange	Lang exchange				Film
17:00							
18:00							
19:00							
20:00							
21:00	Flashcards	Flashcards	Flashcards	Flashcards	Flashcards	Flashcards	Flashcards
22:00	Read	Read	Read	Read	Read	Read	Read
23:00	Diary	Diary	Diary	Diary	Diary	Diary	Diary

Fig 3. My language learning timetable

Don't be tempted to clutter it up with other stuff like work and shopping and secret freemason meetings. Its objective is to focus, remind and motivate. If you're serious about learning, you'll have stuff programmed throughout the whole day—in the mornings, afternoons and evenings. Big things like 90-minute study periods and lots of little things like two minutes of revision.[53]

On your timetable you'll also have your language exchange sessions (the one-to-ones and group meetings), your periods of reading, watching video or listening activities.

53- If you haven't yet grasped the power of doing lots and lots of little activities, then reread the first chapters.

Once you've got your initial timetable sketched out, consider the hierarchy of each activity. You must have a respectable number of higher-end activities scheduled. It might make you nervous, but language learning is all about getting out of your comfort zone and stretching yourself. You must have regular conversation practice with other human beings every week (preferably every day) if you are going to learn your chosen language effectively.

By preparing your timetable, you are committing yourself to the journey you have to take to get from where you are to where you want to be. By putting all your programmed activities into one place, you can start to see how they are all beginning to form a powerful picture: how they are all pieces of the jigsaw puzzle which is slowly but steadily starting to take shape.

After you've tweaked your timetable enough to have it in a state you're happy with, copy it and print it off.[54] The reason for this is, as you go through the week, you're going to cross off each activity as you do it. This gives you that little prize of satisfaction of visually having accomplished each activity and being annoyingly reminded of those you didn't.

Then stick the timetable somewhere where you're going to see it regularly every day which in itself will serve as a Pointer, calling your attention to what has to be done.

Don't forget to include "Change this finished timetable for next week" and keep your pre-printed copies and a roll of Sellotape handy.

Don't be afraid to continue to amend and improve your timetable. It's there to help you, not to make your life unbearable. There's no harm in shuffling things around and adding or substituting one activity for another. So long as you're getting the job done, little by little, that's absolutely fine.

I like timetables. They bring structure and discipline to a project. But I'm well aware this doesn't go for everyone. You might be the sort of person who shudders at the idea of having to stick to a timetable. It's too controlling, too limiting, too unrealistic to fit in with their lifestyle.

54- Unless you like the idea of drawing up exactly the same timetable each week.

This is fine. A fixed timetable isn't necessary so long as you are getting the job done little by little each day. One solution to this problem is what I call the Habit Farm.

The Habit Farm

A farm is somewhere where crops are grown. Little seeds of possibility are planted and then slowly nurtured into life, growing, developing, slowly taking root until finally blossoming into something big and beautiful that can be harvested for the benefit of those who are hungry for it.

A Habit Farm is no different. Here, the little seeds of possibility are the ideas of the habits we want to cultivate. We give them the attention they need: Prizes, Progress, Passion, Peer Pressure and Pointers. And with a little bit of Patience and Positivity (we'll be talking about those a bit later) we slowly start to see our habits taking shape, becoming established and firmly taking root in your normal daily routines.

Here's how it works.

Get a sheet of paper and draw up a grid of 32 columns by about 15 rows. The first column needs to be wide enough to write the little habit you want to plant. About 6cm should do it. The other columns represent the days of the month (31 max.) and can be much narrower (about 0.7cm should be fine). At the top of the first column write the title 'My New Habits' and at the top of columns 2 to 32, write the numbers 1 to 31. These columns represent the days of the month.

Now, at the beginning of each row, under the title of 'My New Habits', you write down what little habit you want to carry out every day. Examples could be:

- Doing at least one exercise in your study book
- Reading at least one page of a story
- Practising your pronunciation for at least a minute
- Learning the lyrics of at least one line of a song
- Doing at least one revision session on AnkiApp

- Making at least one revision card
- Talking for at least five minutes
- Spending at least a minute reading your favourite Role Model's blog

At the end of each day you fill in the corresponding column by writing in your numerical evaluation of how well you've done today. If you haven't done that habit today – zero points. If you've done exceptionally well - give yourself five. It entirely depends on you, so long as you don't cheat by trying to convince yourself you've done more than you honestly have.

Note: You can also include things that you refrain from doing. For instance - 'Not speaking any English during my language class' or 'Not putting on the subtitles when I watch a film'.

At the beginning of the bottom row you write 'Total'. This is because the bottom row is for adding up all your points for each day. This way you can compare days and see if you're slacking or gaining momentum.

Language Learning Habit Farm

	1	2	3	4	5	6	7	8	9	10	11	12	13	14	15	16	17	18	19	20	21	22	23	24	25	26	27	28	29	30	31
Flashcard revision	1	1	1	1	1	1	1	1	1	1	1	1	1	1	1	1	1	1	1	1	1	1	1	1	1	1	1	1	1	1	1
Read	1	1	1		1	1	1	1			1	1		1	1	1	1			1	1	1	1		1	1			1	1	
Listen to radio	1	1	1	1	1			1	1	1	1	1		1	1	1	1			1	1	1	1	1				1	1	1	
Watch TV series	1	1	1	1	1	1		1	1	1	1	1		1	1	1	1	1	1			1	1	1	1	1			1		1
Making revision card from notes	1	1	1		1	1		1	1	1	1	1	1	1	1	1	1	1	1		1	1	1			1	1		1		
Have a conversation with someone	1	1	1	1	1	1	1	1	1	1	1	1	1	1	1	1	1	1	1	1	1	1	1	1	1	1	1	1	1	1	1
One page from excercise book		1		1	1		1			1	1			1	1		1		1	1			1	1							
Language exchange		1	1		1				1		1			1	1				1	1				1	1					1	1
Language class	1			1				1			1			1			1				1			1			1				
Write diary	1	1	1	1	1	1	1	1	1	1	1	1	1	1	1	1	1	1	1	1	1	1	1	1	1	1	1	1	1	1	1
Word of the day	voltant	aleshores	enguany	quinzena	fulgurar	d'hora	surar	espelma	soca	malgrat	maldestra	suro	encès	sota	desenvolupar	empaitar	veu	aixeta	galleda	gairebé	indret	senzill	senar	aixecar	amagar	endoll	cec	eixuta	malson	ninot	garrepa
Total	8	8	9	7	9	7	4	9	7	7	9	9	6	5	9	9	8	8	8	5	6	9	8	8	8	7	6	5	8	7	7

Fig 4. My Habit Farm

I also found it useful to have a row especially for 'Favourite New Word of the Day'. At bedtime, I would add up my points, usually giving me the satisfying reward of a two-digit number, which confirmed I'd had another successfully productive day.

The Habit Farm is one of my favourite perseverance tools. I've used it to help me with my writing. I've used it to help me lose weight. I still use it to help me keep my life in order—to remind me to do those little daily things such as tidying my desk, getting a bit of exercise, doing a bit of housework and taking my happy pills.[55]

If you keep your Habit Farm going for long enough, you'll begin to see some of these habits becoming part of your normal behaviour.[56] However, regardless of how hard you try, some of your little seedling habits will struggle for survival. Something inside you will resist. Don't force it. If you're starting to develop a reluctance to do a particular habit, scrap it. Your seed has landed on barren ground. Accept it and try a different habit with a better chance of survival.

If you have a Study Buddy, I suggest you get them to keep a Habit Farm, too. There's lots of positive peer pressure in comparing Farms and scores. If you're really daring, you can even promise to post your completed Farm on social media every month to put yourself under even more peer pressure. It's entirely up to you.

But one habit I do recommend growing on your Habit Farm is filling in your Diary.

Filling in Your Diary

When developing a language learning strategy, keeping a diary isn't on the top of anyone's list as far as useful habits are concerned. But the reason I'm including it here is not to help you learn but to help you keep learning. Let me explain.

As we've seen, when learning a new skill, it is important to practise a little bit as often as possible every day. It needs continuous effort. It needs constant motivation. It needs perseverance.

55- That last one is a joke.

56- Not taking sugar in my tea and coffee is one of the benefits I harvested from my Farm.

When things are going well, maintaining your momentum towards your objective is easy: it's like freewheeling downhill. But when things aren't going so well—when your morale is low, when your momentum has ground to a halt, when you feel it's all a waste of time—that's when your spirits need boosting. You need some sort of reward, some sense of progress and some rekindled passion. One source of these is from your Goal Diary. As we saw in chapter 3, your diary, amongst other things, is for recording all your positive experiences, all your breakthroughs, all your successes.

Reading about how relieved you felt after you met your first language exchange partner, or about when you discovered one of your favourite expressions, or how pleased you were to be able to order your first meal in your target language reminds you how far you've come. It helps remind you of all the success you've had and why putting yourself through this is worthwhile.

During those dark moments when you're feeling less than enthusiastic about language learning, you'll try to ignore these details. There'll be a voice inside of you ranting on about how the whole idea is just an unrealistic fantasy. Keeping your language learning Diary can help change all that. It can remind you of all the little but nevertheless important things you've achieved so far. If you write them down, you can't ignore them. They will help refloat your boat and get you sailing again towards your destination.

All of these perseverance tools can help. They might not make a huge difference, but they each make enough of a difference to keep you going forwards. The only thing you need to do now is to make sure your expectations don't start to get ahead of your capabilities. In other words, you have to make sure you have your patience well under control. Why not answer a few questions before considering patience in the next chapter?

Questions

- What projects have you (or someone you know) achieved by carrying out an activity every single day?

- What helped you (or them) do this activity so regularly?

- How many daily activities are you doing at the moment to improve your language learning?

- How could you incorporate a useful new habit into an existing routine?

- Do you think drawing yourself up a weekly timetable would help you focus? What would you have to do to make it work?

- Do you think a Habit Farm could help you cultivate a few benevolent habits? What habits would you have on your farm?

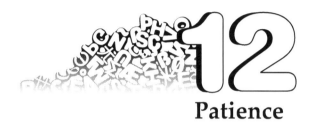

Patience

"The two most powerful warriors are patience and time."

– Leo Tolstoy, Russian novelist

Isabella

Isabella wanted to perfect her English. She had applied for a job that required proficiency level (C2) and yet she had only just passed her First Certificate (C1) a couple of months before. She decided to do a month's immersion course in Warwick and she eagerly forked out a small fortune. But, although her English did improve, she didn't pass her proficiency exam. She didn't get the job. She felt frustrated and a failure.

As far as I'm concerned, Isabella is a keen and capable student. Her problem was not her ability, nor was it her progress; she was improving her English fluency perfectly respectably.

Her problem was her patience.

It's really, really important you start with a realistic grasp of what you're asking of yourself. You can't start a new language on the Monday morning and expect to be a capably fluent speaker by Friday afternoon. By expecting too much too soon, your little adventure is guaranteed to end in disappointment.

There are books out there that promise to teach you how to speak a new language in 3 months, or 21 days or even just a week. If you're going to seriously consider buying one of these books, look carefully at what the book is promising: the author's definition of 'speaking a new language' and yours might not be the same.

Secondly, identify what the book is asking of you. If it expects your undivided attention 24/7 when the best you can spare is 30 minutes a day, then the goods are not going to be delivered on time. I don't doubt for a minute you can become functionally competent in a 'user-friendly' language in just 3 months, providing you have the time. It's fair to say you need a word base of 1000+ for basic communication. One thousand words learnt in 3 months means learning 11 new words per day, every day, in addition to pronunciation, structures and genders.

The trick to being patient is not just to do with being realistic—it's to do with focus. By this, I mean how often you choose to think about your objective. Even if 1000 words is realistic for your situation, it can still look like a very big figure when you're struggling to learn your first fifty.

If you're just starting out as a beginner, when you see a video of a native speaker in full flow, the distance between where you are now and where you want to be is so immense it is practically begging for the feeling of frustration and despondency to come a calling.

Looking to the distant horizon may serve to keep you heading in the right direction but you need to keep your attention fixed on the task you have immediately ahead of you. If today you're going to learn a few useful expressions involving parts of the body, then do just that and be satisfied with a job well done at the end of the day.

We looked at the importance of milestones in chapter 7.7. Milestones are great for dealing with impatience. Instead of thinking about your final objective, focus on getting to your next milestone. Whatever it is, it'll be much closer and much more achievable than your long-term Goal.

Don't get caught in the trap of 'so many words, so little time'. Yes, I agree every language has hundreds of thousands of words. But so what? You don't need to learn all of them. You don't need to know 100% of a language to be able to speak it. Not even if you want to get to proficiency level. Even if you're a native English speaker, you are unlikely to know even a quarter of the words in the English language.

Misosophist, lucubration, zeugma, scurryfunge and persiflage are all English words and yet if you can correctly define any of them I'd be impressed.[57]

In fact, even though there are over 170,000 words in the Oxford English Dictionary (with over 600,000 definitions) the experts estimate the average person only knows about 20,000 to 30,000 words. What's more, the number of different words used by the average person on a daily basis is even less, just a few thousand. So by learning just 3000 words you can get by in any language most of the time.

Even with a vocabulary of just 1000, it is still possible to have meaningful and persiflageous conversations if you try.

Focus on Progress

Another way to combat impatience is to look at your Progress Plotter. If you remember, your Progress Plotter is the graph you plot every day or every week by counting the number of revision cards you've learnt.

When you draw up your Progress Plotter at the beginning, you start by marking where you are to begin at the bottom left and where you want to get to at the top right. The straight red line you draw connecting these two points represents your intended line of progress. So long as the points you plot every day or every week stay close to this line (preferably above it) then you are on track and doing absolutely fine.

57- Misosophist: a person who hates wisdom; Lucubration: a prolonged period of writing or study; Zeugma: a figure of speech in which a word applies to two others in different senses (e.g. John and his driving licence expired last week); Scurryfunge: to rush around cleaning when company is on their way over; Persiflage: good-natured banter.

Instead of looking at your Goal, which probably seems like a long way away, look at your line of intended progress. Find the date for next week along the bottom axis. From that point, move your finger up until it reaches the line. That point indicates the progress you need to have made in the next seven days. It won't seem anywhere near as daunting as what you still need to do to achieve your end Goal. If all is going well, what you need to achieve to meet your progress requirements for next week should be perfectly manageable. And that's fine for the moment. The only thing you need to concern yourself with is to make sure you put in what's needed today to take the next modest step necessary to stay up above the line by the end of the week.

If plotting graphs aren't your thing, another way of dealing with patience is, once more, to go back to your Goal Diary. All being well, you'll have written down a few notes about things you've learnt, progress you've made and the positive experiences you've had. When you're feeling impatient, look back through your diary to remind yourself of how far you've come along.

So by all means, be ambitious in your language learning, but realistically so. Patiently does it. If you can see you're making steady progress, enjoy what you're doing, have plenty of positive peer pressure and have established several daily habits which are working well, then all that is required is for you to focus on what you can realistically achieve for the moment.

With good solid habits, steady progress and your patience under control, your language learning venture is almost guaranteed. But there is one final occurrence you need to be prepared for. At some point in the not too distant future, you're going to get a visitor. Who this visitor is and why they want to mess up your plans is what we'll be looking at in the next chapter. But why not answer some questions first?

Questions

- Can you remember when a lack of patience caused you problems?

- What could you have done to help?

- Do you feel impatient about your language learning?

- How can you increase your focus onto short-term goals? Which short-term goals?

- Could a Progress Plotter help?

- Do you have any other ways to improve your patience?

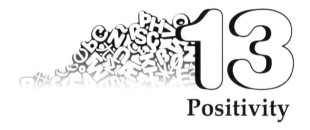

Positivity

"In language learning it is attitude not aptitude that determines success."

– Steve Kaufman, author of *The Way of the Linguist*

General Futility

When you're having a good day, it's easy to feel good about yourself. When you're calm, relaxed and in control of things, it's easy to approach the tasks in your life with a practical go-for-it optimism. It's time to learn a language or build the shed or save the world. Great! Let's do it!

But not all days are good days. You might be having a particularly stressful time at work. You might have had an especially frustrating language exchange. You might even have gone through your revision cards and for some reason found you know less now than you did last week.[58]

58- Don't worry about this. It happens. It's called Temporary Stupidity. Trust me, it doesn't last.

You're thinking about your new language when suddenly, there's a knock at the door. You answer it to find a short, sour-faced little man in a military uniform, cigar in mouth, angrily staring up at you.

"What on earth do you think you're doing?" he barks. "Language learning? What a load of crap! It won't work! Can't you see? Are you blind as well as stupid?! You're not a linguist! You haven't got a clue! You're only fooling yourself! You are never going succeed! It's all a complete and utter WASTE OF TIME!"

You get the idea, don't you?

This character is called General Futility. He likes to visit when you're feeling down, when your positivity is low.

The General doesn't just attack your language learning; he pours derision on everything you do. I speak from experience—very recent experience in fact. Just yesterday, the General came to call. He often comes on rainy days and yesterday was very rainy. Nobody but the perversely optimistic feels good about getting up when it's dark, cold and pissing it down and that's exactly how yesterday started. To exacerbate the situation further, the rain had enlisted the help of a particularly vindictive wind that blew the rain into your face and your brolly inside out just when you were trying to stop the kids from jumping into yet another muddy puddle.

Adding insult to injury, the plumber who was supposed to be coming round to fix the blocked sink (probably due to the kids stuffing a hamster down it or something similar) phoned at an inopportune moment to say he was going to stay at home instead. And from there on the door was just wide open, practically begging for General Futility to come and visit. And lo and behold... there he was!

After I'd dried myself off from installing the kids in their place of educational enlightenment, I tried to sit down and write. But nothing came out. Not even making myself a cup of tea made a difference. I found myself thinking "Who's going to be interested in another book on language learning? There's loads of good books out there written by people who speak far more languages than me."

But at the same time, I was able to recognise the situation. I could tell my positivity had dipped and I'm now wise enough to know that when it does it's just temporary. On the days you feel down, the best thing you can do is just ride it out. It will pass. That was yesterday. Today is better: It's still cold but the rain has passed and the sun is shining. I had a coffee with an old friend Anne, who I'd recently bumped into at a conference. I told her all about my work, my ideas and my writing and she thought it was marvellous and made me promise to let her know when this next book comes out. Furthermore, I got a couple of messages this morning, one from a colleague called Mario asking me to help him with a presentation he has to give and another friend and partner in crime, Patricia, who had some good news about a project we're working on together.

Here I am now. Back from the doldrums feeling absolutely fine again. My positivity has been recharged and I'm feeling all the better for it. I'm looking forward to my target-language bedtime reading and going through my revision cards.

Be aware of your positivity level. Just like your smartphone needs to be regularly recharged, so do you. But instead of electrical power, you need to be recharged with positivity.

This can happen naturally. A nice walk, a beautiful view, a smile from a stranger or a hug from a friend. They can all do wonders to improve our mood.[59]

In addition, there are lots of activities we've looked at so far that can help you recharge. If you cast your mind back to the previous chapters, you just might be able to remember a few.

What Your Goal Diary Is For

Your Goal Diary can be an excellent source of positivity. Somewhere at the beginning of it, you'll have written down all the reasons why you chose to

---

59- It's worth pointing out these activities have a lasting effect on our mood. The positive effect can last for hours and are perfectly healthy. But there are some things we do to make ourselves feel better for just a short period of time that are not so healthy. Smoking, alcohol, drugs and comfort food all fit into this category.

study your target language in the first place. Take a moment to carefully go through these, visualising each one. Is each reason still valid, or have circumstances changed? Just like Charlie in Case Study 3, are there any new reasons that have popped up? If so, add them in.

But the Positivity top-ups you can get from your Diary don't stop there. Your Goal Diary should also be filled with all the positive experiences you've had regarding your linguistic journey. You'll have been including how good each one of these made you feel at the time. Going through these moments help bring back the positive feelings that General Futility would rather have you forget. It's much harder to make yourself believe it's all a waste of time if you have concrete evidence to the contrary.

Finally, your Goal Diary should have records of your Progress. We looked at the importance of Progress in chapter 7 which hopefully you've been measuring regularly, especially if you've been using a Progress Plotter. The strength of these measurements is they are irrefutable evidence that your language learning is going in the right direction. It's not wishful thinking. It's not some fanciful dream. It's you, steadily learning your new language. The General would have you believe you're not making any progress at all, but the facts will clearly say otherwise.

The General at some point will play the 'not for much longer' card. He'll point out that, "Okay, okay, so you might be making a bit of trivial progress at the moment, but it can't go on for much longer. You never made much progress with your previous attempts. This language learning lark is not for you. You're not cut out for it. You'll become a laughing stock. Why not quit while you're ahead and still have your dignity intact?"

The reason why people fail is because they give up, which is exactly what the General wants. If you've learned two hundred words so far, there is absolutely no reason why you can't learn another two hundred. The more you learn, the easier it becomes to learn more still. Each new piece of language forms a foundation to support the next.

The suggestion you can only remember so much and then not have room for anything else is complete nonsense. It's not a question of remembering, it's a question of learning. Once you've learnt a word or expression, you don't have to remember it any more. It's fixed there. It's just like swimming. When you jump in the pool you don't try to remember how to do it—you just do it. Language is the same.

Positivity from People

If you're struggling to reconcile these feelings, your next option is to talk to someone. Consider all the people giving you positive peer pressure. When you're running out of positivity, share how you feel with your language group, your language exchange partner or your teacher/tutor. It's more than likely they've gone through something similar.

Praise Donors are another great source of positivity. Go and have a drink with your Praise Donor and cry on their shoulder for a bit. You'll feel better for getting things off your chest. If you've chosen the right person, their inevitable response will be to point out you're doing better than you think. Slow and steady gets the job done. You can do this if you keep at it. After all, Rome wasn't built in a day.

Rome wasn't built in a day. If this expression resonates, your lack of positivity might be due to a lack of patience. You're spending too much time thinking about your long-term goal and not enough about what you can achieve right now.

Focus on your immediate objectives: to practise speaking with your exchanges, to read for pleasure, to write down important new expressions and to make a few revision cards and go over them several times a day. That's plenty to do in one week. If you focus on your short-term goals, you'll stop focussing on your long-term goals which are causing you anxiety and draining your positivity levels.

Silver Linings

Every cloud has a silver lining, as they say.

General Futility is very good at pointing out all the bad points that inevitably arise during your language learning adventure. What's more, he makes absolutely no effort whatsoever to mention the counterbalancing good ones. In fact, the General will do everything in his power to cover up anything positive. He'll deny its very existence.

The positive sides are there. You just need to let someone draw attention to them.

When I was little, I remember grazing my knee. It hurt a lot. My mum took me to the bathroom, sat me down and, after cleaning the wound, put some antiseptic lotion on it. If I thought it hurt beforehand, that was nothing compared to what I experienced with the antiseptic. It stung like hell! But my mum explained the antiseptic was made up of lots of tiny soldiers which at that very moment were fighting off the nasty dirty things that had got into the wound. She told me the pain was a good thing—all part of the process of curing the wound and saving me from a gangrenous amputation. That made the whole thing seem more bearable. It was her way of showing me a positive view of the situation.

And as far as language learning goes, if you'll allow me, I'd like to show you mine.

Negative: It's too difficult.
Positive: No language is 'difficult', as millions of native speakers prove. A new language just needs time to be absorbed. You don't study a language. You just need to be exposed to it, to experience it and to keep practising it. If you're feeling your language is too difficult, it's probably because a) you're not getting enough exposure/practice and b) you're expecting too much, too soon. Reread the previous chapter on Patience.

Negative: I'm too old.
Positive: No, no, no. My father was studying Italian when he shuffled off his mortal coil. He was 79. We know senior citizens can learn new language because there are many of them who do so. They've even done brain-scans that show the neuroplasticity of the brains of octogenarians— or in other words: our brains are still capable of learning right to the end. You're never too old.

Negative: I'm too stupid.
Positive: If you're stupid at anything, it's at understanding the concept of you not needing to be intelligent to learn a language. You just need to

practise enough. Would you say you were too stupid to learn to swim or ride a bike? You don't need to 'understand' a language any more than you need to understand fluid dynamics to learn the breaststroke.

Negative: I sound like a wally.

Positive: No, you don't. You sound EXACTLY the same as everyone else who's started out learning it. You can't learn to run before you can walk and, unfortunately, you can't learn to walk before you learn to slowly drag yourself along the carpet. It's a necessary part of the process. When you begin learning a language you're going to sound like a beginner. Accept it. It proves you've got the balls to make the effort.

Negative: I get embarrassed.

Positive: You are stepping out of your comfort zone. Welcome to a bigger world. Outside your comfort zone, you're going to feel insecure, frightened and uncomfortable. Brilliant! You're learning something. The more times you do it and the longer you bear it, the more you'll learn and the easier it gets. Good for you. Embrace embarrassment. It's a good sign you're doing it right.

Negative: I make lots of mistakes.

Positive: Good! Just like sounding like a wally and getting embarrassed, it shows you're trying. It shows you're stretching yourself. This is important. It took the Wright Brothers thousands of attempts to build a 'right' aeroplane. You could say they made thousands of mistakes but I think 'thousands of attempts' is fairer. You're not making a mistake, you're making an effort. You're making your first attempts at getting your new language off the ground and soaring into the air.

Negative: I don't have the time.

Positive: This isn't you talking. It's General Futility pulling the strings and moving your mouth. If someone was in the centre of town giving out big fat bundles of fifty-pound notes, would you find time to get up off your arse and go and get a couple of carrier-bags full? If you can make time for that, you can find 5 minutes here and 10 minutes there to learn something useful. I'm sure a total of 30 minutes scraped together throughout the day would be possible.

Negative: I can't afford it.

Positive: There is so much free stuff available on the internet it'll make your head spin. If you are so financially limited you haven't got access to the worldwide web or a public library and you live in one of those small secluded villages where making contact with other people only happens during the mating season, then yes, okay, you may be right. But if you have a smartphone, if you have broadband, then no—you can afford it because the cost is almost free.

Negative: It's boring.

Positive: Most likely you think this because learning a language at school was boring: textbooks, grammar, pointless exercises, painful exams, failed grades and being bottom of the class.[60] Of course it was boring. The experts don't learn languages like that either because it's boring for them, too. The way to learn best is to play about with the language. Enjoy it. Experience it in whatever way you like best. You don't need grammar, you don't need to learn all the conjugations. Just do stuff that interests you and enjoy yourself.

As they say, you can lead a horse to water but you cannot make it drink. You could force yourself to look at a 'Teach Yourself' book, sit in front of the telly, hear the sound of a recording. But if you don't have a positive attitude to learning, if your mind isn't open to the idea, if you don't approach your project with a can-do mentality then you're giving yourself a tremendous handicap right from the start.

Find the way that works for you to sort out your positivity. It'll be worth it.

60- Remember, I'm still speaking from experience. This was me when I was fourteen.

Questions

- Think of the last time you had a 'bad day'. How did it affect you?

- How does a low positivity level generally change your behaviour?

- What do you usually do (if anything) to cheer yourself up?

- Is it one of the healthy ones?

- What else could you do?

- How could you increase the chances of you using a new 'pick-me-up' method the next time you're feeling down?

- On a scale of 1 to 10, how would you grade your attitude to learning your language at the moment?

- What could you do to improve it?

- If you still don't know, who could you talk to for inspiration?

Case Study 4: Ian

Brenda (Case Study 1) had a solid group of Study Buddies; Charlie (Case Study 2) had the time and the money to study; and Anne (Case Study 3) had lots of French-speaking family to practise with. But I count my close friends on the fingers of one hand and they are all very busy people, none of whom are interested in studying my target language. My own timetable was pretty full already, thank you very much, and I'm loathed to spend money when it's not necessary. And even though I live in Barcelona, I don't have lots of relatives queuing up to practice with me. It was clear whatever techniques I was to employ, they were going to be very different. Here's a summary of what I did.

- I had three Goals: to pass my Catalan exam in June; to give a 10-minute presentation in July; and to be able to learn enough about different language learning techniques to be able to write this book.

- I identified all my reasons for why I wanted to do this. Occasionally, I'd consult them, imagining what benefits and rewards success would bring.

- I listened to the radio for thirty minutes on my way to and from work. Fortunately, there are lots of local radio stations just dedicated to chitchat. I had lots to choose from. I'd listen for useful phrases and repeat them out loud a few times to get my mouth round them.

- I read most evenings. I was quite proud of myself when I found I was able to read literature, albeit children's literature. I started with 'The Triplets' books (*Tres Bessones)* and worked my way up from there.

- My bedtime routine also included playing the gamified apps. I tried Memrize and Quizlet but I found them a bit slow and laborious (though for beginners they're probably ideal). I settled on Duolingo which was faster.

- I also became a big, big fan of AnkiApp. I used it a lot. I still do. Not just for language learning but for other stuff I have to learn. I put the Anki icon onto my phone's home screen. It is always there as a Pointer. At every opportunity I'd do a minute's revision of ten cards. Especially while waiting. I can't help but notice the amount of people on the metro who are on their phones playing games or texting. How much could these people achieve if they spent their daily commute learning something instead?[61]

- I tried to get speaking practice every day. This wasn't as easy as you might think living in Barcelona. I tried attending language groups and sorting out language exchanges, but it was tricky. I developed an unhealthy set of excuses not to interact with such people. I find dealing with strangers stressful enough, even when talking in English. In the end, I was lucky to find a handful of people I could meet with regularly once or twice a week either in the mornings or evenings. I found these conversations to be extremely useful and I strongly recommend making the effort to find language exchanges you get along with. They're interesting, fun and you'll make some good friends.

- What I also found useful was to have conversations with myself. I know this sort of behaviour isn't considered healthy. But I thought the ends justified the means and so I started to do it when I was alone in the house.[62] I found telling fairy-stories to be a good way of practising. I also explained to myself what I'd done that day or what I was going to do the following.

- I kept a Progress Plotter and a Habit Farm. Both of these worked very well for me. I definitely got that much-needed little prize when I filled them in. I still find these two Perseverance tools useful. The Plotter has also become a fundamental tool to help me write. I use the Farm every day to keep my little habits well cultivated and in check. If it weren't for my Habit Farm, my daily exercises, my dietary excesses and my personal organising wouldn't be what they are today.

61- One of the things I've learnt from my language learning adventure is just how much time we waste waiting—for the bathroom to be free, for the kettle to boil, for the kids to get dressed, for the wife to find her keys/phone/glasses, for the lights to turn green, for the computer to boot up, for the bus/train to come, for the meeting to start, for the meeting to end, for the kids to come out of school, for the oven to warm up, for your freshly-made tea to cool down, for the film to start, for any human being at the customer service department to get up off their bloody arse and answer the bloody phone.

62- I strongly recommend against trying to talk to yourself in your target language while you're driving through challenging traffic. It requires much more mental effort and concentration than talking in your native language. When you drive, you must be concentrating on the road.

- I'd say General Futility comes to visit two or three times a month. Sometimes it all seems so difficult and so far away. All the Positivity recommendations I've given in chapter 13 are things I've used myself[63] and they all work. My Goal Diary and my Progress Plotter are especially useful in such times. I also find talking to family and friends for moral support a great help.

I successfully sat my Catalan B1 exam a month earlier than expected, in May 2017. Two months after that, I gave my 10-minute talk in Catalan entitled '*El que vaig aprendre d'aprendre un idioma*' (What I learnt from learning a language). Looking back, it's quite probably the most nerve-wracking thing I've ever done. Fortunately, it all went smoothly. But I've never felt so nervous and then so relieved in my entire life.

The whole process of going from being unable to string two coherent sentences together to being able to pass an exam and give a presentation (without using notes) took me six months. For someone who didn't like learning languages, I don't think that's too bad. I finished this book three months later, the following September.

63- Come to think of it, mostly all of the recommendations I've given in all the chapters I've used myself.

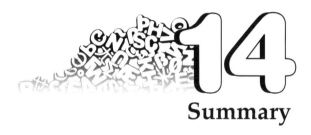

Summary

*"To God I speak Spanish, to women Italian, to men French, and to my horse —
German."*

– Emperor Charles V, ruler of the Spanish and Holy Roman Empires

Towards the end of writing this book, I was asked which language had
been easier for me to learn, Spanish or Catalan?

Without hesitation, my reply was Catalan.

Critics would point out this is not surprising as Catalan is a Romance
language just like Spanish is, so knowing how to speak one language
helps understand the second. This is true. But my answer was more based
on how I felt about the *process* of studying each language.

All those years back when I started Spanish, I really didn't have much of
a clue what I was doing. I had a couple of books (Spanish grammar and
a 'Teach Yourself Spanish') and I remember forking out a small fortune

for a series of cassettes you were supposed to listen to and absorb as you drifted off to sleep.

But looking back, I mostly remember feeling frustrated and lost. I had no idea what I was supposed to be doing. I had very little sense of progress, I had no strategy and certainly no structure. My studying was sporadic, half-hearted and totally unsatisfactory. I read my grammar book hoping it would somehow do me some good. Nobody explained the importance of paying attention to pronunciation. I felt completely lost in a confusing jungle of incomprehensible language without any clear idea of which way to go. In hindsight, I acquired my Spanish in spite of my attempts to study it. I'm sure 99% of my Spanish came from living alongside Spanish speakers and interacting with them every day.

If I felt lost in the jungle with my Spanish, then in contrast, my Catalan learning has been a promenade through the park.

In addition to the actual language, what I have learnt these last six months is how useful and psychologically important having a structure can be. At no point did I feel lost or confused. Starting from the beginning, the process, the 'day-to-day'ness of learning was clear and easy. Discovering I didn't need to go anywhere near a grammar book was a luxury. Not having to learn a hundred irregular verbs by rote was another dream come true.

The suggestions, advice and recommendations of the language learning gurus is all valid – if you're a language enthusiast. I started this journey with trepidation, not really sure how it was going to work out. But the more I carried out my daily actions, the more I found myself enjoying it, which, to be honest, I found pleasantly surprising. Most of the activities (language exchanges with friendly people, reading for pleasure and going through notes and revision cards) were enjoyable and fulfilling. The ones I didn't enjoy (such as the language exchange group) I dropped and replaced with something else.

Having clear objectives with clear deadlines gave me focus and motivation to keep making the effort. Being able to see my constant progress was a strong motivator as was referring to my Goal Diary to remember all the ups, not just the downs.

It only makes me wonder, if I had known 30 years ago what I know now about language learning, how much of a difference would it have made to my life?

What about you? If you're reading this book because you're learning a language or interested in doing so, what have you got from these pages that you can take away and apply? What will your strategy be to become a successful language learner and once you've achieved that? Where will it take you?

I'm sure it will be somewhere wonderful.

So put your language learning backpack on. Stuff it full of the tricks, tips and techniques you've picked from these pages (plus those you've discovered for yourself) and set off on your adventure. May it be fulfilling. May it be rewarding and may it be successful.

All the best and happy language learning!

Appendices

A: Language Levels

Languages are complicated. How fluent someone is can be a debatable point. Nevertheless, in order to try to have some sort of benchmarks, the Common European Framework of Reference for Languages (CEFRL) was set up in the early 1990s in a valiant effort to gauge whether everyone else agrees with your claim that you are at a certain level.

Beginner

You can understand and use simple expressions and predictable phrases such as 'Hello' and 'One beer, please'.

You can answer simple questions about yourself, such as where you live and things you like such as dogs and tea.

You can only interact with another person if they talk slowly and are prepared to be very patient with you.

You might know a couple of rude words but you're unsure about how to use them.

Elementary

You can understand sentences and common expressions related to basic subjects (e.g. shopping, local geography and relationships).

You can carry out simple or routine tasks that don't require complicated conversation on predictable matters (e.g. acquiring alcohol, ascertaining the location of the nearest sanitary facilities and apologising).

You can talk a bit about your personal background, your present situation and stuff you need (e.g. warmth, food, an adapter to recharge your phone).

You know a handful of rude words and are able to use them when provoked.

Intermediate

You can understand the main points of normal user-friendly language.

You can deal with most situations likely to arise while travelling in an area where the language is spoken.

You can write simple sentences about familiar concepts or things of interest.

You can describe experiences and events, dreams, hopes and ambitions.

You can briefly justify your actions to members of the local law enforcement body.

You know most of the common taboo words and can use them in predictable circumstances.

Upper Intermediate

You can read normal texts and get the main idea as well as detailed information.

You can talk to people reasonably fluently without them getting frustrated.

You can write about most things (real or abstract), justifying your opinions.

You can competently insult people in a variety of ways and incorporate expletives into normal conversation.

Advanced

You can understand most complicated language of a predictable nature.

You can express yourself fluently and spontaneously without having to search for expressions.

You can converse socially, academically and professionally.

You can write well about complicated stuff.

You have a broad knowledge of rude words and expressions which you can use fluently in the appropriate situations.

Proficiency

You can understand with ease virtually everything heard or read.

You can write about anything you want in a totally natural way.

You can talk in the same way as native speakers do. People think you're a native.

You can swear, insult and use expletives, taboo words and invent your own profanities in a totally natural and creative way.

B: Languages According to Difficulty

Even though I still firmly stand by my statement that 'hours of study' are not an accurate indication of how much language you are learning, it's still being used worldwide until somebody can come up with a better universal standard.

If we start off by assuming you're a native English speaker, then some foreign languages are going to be relatively easy to learn. For instance,

Scouse, Geordie, Glaswegian and Broad Yorkshire are all very closely related to Standard English and can be mastered with just a few weeks of study (20 hours). Esperanto speakers claim it's such an easy language it can be learnt in just 150 hours.

But most other languages need several hundred hours of study/practise to absorb them completely. According to the current trend, there are four or five groups, depending on whether you want to isolate German into a group of its own. Here they are.[64]

Group 1: (about 600 hours). This level is for languages that have close connections to English. It is estimated that the average person could reach proficiency after about 600 hours of study.

Afrikaans

Catalan

Danish

Dutch

French

Italian

Norwegian

Portuguese

Romanian

Spanish

Swedish

Group 2: I've nothing against the Germans but the experts claim it needs a level all to itself and another 150 hours to master. That means gaining proficiency at 750 hours.

German

Group 3: This level is for is for languages that have some major differences with English, either linguistically or culturally. For this group you'll need about 900 hours to become proficient.

64- Source: http://www.effectivelanguagelearning.com/language-guide/language-difficulty

Indonesian
Malaysian
Swahili

Group 4: In this group you have languages that are substantially different from English. Consider yourself very lucky if you can master any of them in less than 1100 hours.

Albanian
Amharic
Armenian
Azerbaijani
Bengali
Bosnian
Bulgarian
Burmese
Croatian
Czech
*Estonian
*Finnish
*Georgian
Greek
Hebrew
Hindi
*Hungarian
Icelandic
Khmer
Lao
Latvian
Lithuanian
Macedonian
*Mongolian
Nepali
Pashto

Persian (Dari, Farsi, Tajik)

Polish

Russian

Serbian

Sinhala

Slovak

Slovenian

Tagalog

*Thai

Turkish

Ukrainian

Urdu

Uzbek

*Vietnamese

Xhosa

Zulu

Group 5: This group is for those languages that are so weird and wonderful they are considered notoriously difficult and need over twice the time of the previous group and almost four times more study than Group 1. Expect to be studying this group for most of the rest of your foreseeable future (about 2400 hours) in order to become proficient.

Arabic

Cantonese

Mandarin

*Japanese

Korean

* Languages with an asterisk are a bit more difficult for native English speakers.

C: How to Improve Your Pronunciation

Pronunciation is as important as vocabulary. Think of what it was like the last time you heard someone speaking English who hadn't bothered to master the correct pronunciation.

In the simplest terms, when you speak your target language, you must impersonate the accent of that language, too.

- Pay particular attention to the unusual or difficult sounds. Discover how your mouth has to move in weird and wonderful ways to reproduce these new sounds. Notice if the language tends to be produced more from the front of the mouth, the back of the throat or through the nose. Accept that's the way it's done, cooperate and practise it that way.

- Get used to it. Expose yourself to the sound of your new language as much as possible. Even if you don't understand a word, you can still get used to the 'feel' of it.

- With the more challenging languages, don't shirk from physical linguistic exercises. If some particular phoneme feels unnatural and uncomfortable, it's because you're not used to it. By repeating it a few dozen times every day, you'll gradually find the unnatural starts to feel more friendly and familiar.

- Have you ever heard a recording of yourself speaking? Did it surprise you? How we think we sound and how we actually sound can be two very different things. Explore this for yourself. Record yourself speaking your new language and see how you sound. Are you convincing?

- Don't think that by speaking quickly you're speaking fluently. It's much better to pronounce a new word slowly but correctly and then build up a bit of fluency later. A decent speed of delivery will come in good time.

- Ask for help. If you're struggling with certain pronunciations, or if you're not sure about whether what you're doing is right, get some supportive feedback from a sympathetic native speaker. Ask them directly about your pronunciation and how you can improve.

In short, accept the fact that not only are you going to learn to speak a new language, you're also going to learn to speak it with the right accent, too, no matter how funny it might sound to start with.

D: Most Useful First Phrases

If you're just starting to learn your target language, here is a list of the most useful kinds of expressions you can learn. Just pop them into your translation app and off you go!

1. Hello/Good morning/afternoon, etc.
2. My name is [insert name here].
3. What's your name?
4. How are you?
5. I'm fine, thanks.
6. I'm learning [insert language here].
7. I've been studying for [insert duration here].
8. Excuse me.
9. Do you speak [insert language here]?
10. I'm sorry.
11. I don't understand.
12. What did you say?
13. Can you say that again, please?
14. How do you say [insert word here]?
15. How do you spell that?
16. Could you speak more slowly, please?
17. Thank you very much.
18. You are very kind/patient.
19. See you later.
20. Goodbye.
21. I have [insert concept here, e.g. a headache].
22. Do you have [insert concept here]?
23. Do you like [insert concept here]?
24. Yes, I like it. No, I don't like it.
25. What do you think?
26. I'm from [insert location here].
27. Where are you from?
28. I live in [insert location here].
29. Where do you live?
30. Where are the gents'/ladies' toilets?

E: Common Conversation Structures

When we first learn a language, our tendency is to start learning nouns and verbs. But when we want to talk to someone in real life, it's not because we want to tell them what the cat is doing on the mat. It's more likely because we want to do something. We want to attain, explain or complain. To do this, we need what is known as 'functional' language. Here is a list of the sort of useful functions (along with a couple of examples) that will serve you well if you want to talk to real people in real situations.

Accepting a suggestion
- That's great.
- Good idea.

Advising
- If I were you, I'd…
- I think you should…

Agreeing
- I agree.
- I think you're right.

Apologising
- I'm sorry.
- I didn't realise…

Approving
- I like that.
- Very good.

Asking for clarification
- What do you mean?
- Could you explain a bit more?

Asking for help
- Can you help me, please?
- Could you …, please?

Asking for information
- Could you tell me…?
- I'd like to know…

Asking for permission
- Can I ...?
- Is it alright if...?

Asking for repetition
- What did you say?
- Could you say that again?

Checking their comprehension
- Do you understand me?
- Do you see what I mean?

Checking your comprehension
- Do you mean to say...?
- So what you're saying is...

Denying permission
- I'm afraid not.
- I'm sorry but...

Disagreeing
- I don't agree.
- That's not true.

Doubting
- I'm not sure...
- Maybe...

Dismissing a point
- It doesn't matter.
- That's not important.

Expressing certainty
- I'm sure.
- Definitely.

Expressing disbelief
- I don't believe it!
- Well I never!

Expressing lack of knowledge
- I don't know.
- I've no idea.

Expressing lack of understanding
- I don't understand.
- I don't know what you mean.

Expressing preference
- I prefer…
- I'd much rather…

Expressing surprise
- Good grief!
- Oh my God!

Guessing
- Maybe…
- Could it be…?

Inviting
- Would you like to …?
- I'd like to invite you to…

Offering help
- Would you like me to…?
- Can I …?

Offering something
- Would you like …?
- Could I offer you …?

Stalling for time
- That's a good question.
- Let me think.

Suggesting
- Why don't I/you/we…?
- How about…?

Summarising
- So what you're saying is…
- In other words…

Sympathising
- What a pity.
- I'm so sorry.

F: References and recommended sources

Noteworthy Websites

There are many, many varied and wonderful websites on language learning. Here are a few of my favourite that seem to crop up time after time.

- http://www.bbc.co.uk/languages/

- http://www.fluentin3months.com

- http://www.fluentlanguage.co.uk

- http://www.fluentu.com

- http://www.italki.com

- http://www.iwillteachyoualanguage.com

- http://www.l2mastery.com

- http://www.livelingua.com

- http://www.mezzoguild.com

- http://www.omniglot.com

- http://www.openculture.com

- http://www.polyglotclub.com

Noteworthy Books

- *Babel No More: The Search for the World's Most Extraordinary Language Learners* by Michael Erard

- *Fluent in 3 Months* by Benny Lewis

- *Fluent Forever* by Gabriel Wyner

- *How To Learn Any Language: Quickly, Easily, Inexpensively, Enjoyably and on Your Own* by Barry Farber

- *Polyglot: How I Learn Languages* by Kató Lomb

- *The Cambridge Encyclopaedia of Language* by David Crystal

- *The Language Instinct* by Steven Pinker (not so much a language learning book, more a book on how our brain is built for language learning. Nevertheless, absolutely fascinating)

- *The Study of Language* by George Yule

- *The Way of the Linguist* by Steve Kaufman

Ted Talks

If you want to build up your motivation, I thoroughly recommend watching these:

Benny Lewis: *Hacking language learning*

Chris Lonsdale: *How to learn any language in six months*

Claudio Santori & Muezz Vestin: *Secret to hack a country and learn language for free*

Dr. Conor Quinn: *Hacking language learning Gaston Dorren: Grow up, learn another language*

John McWhorter: *4 reasons to learn a new language*

John Sloan: *Learn language emotionally*

Matthew Youlden: *How to learn any language easily*

Scott Young & Vat Jaiswal: *One simple method to learn any language*

Sid Efromvich: *5 techniques to speak any language*

Tim Doner: *Breaking the language barrier*

Language Learning in One Page

- Decide what your language learning **GOAL** is and write it down.

- After that, write down all your **REASONS** for learning it.

- Keep a **GOAL DIARY**.

- Establish **MILESTONES** that can be achieved within a few weeks of each other.

- Follow the **20 LAWS** of Language Learning.

- Choose your favourite **PIECES** of your language learning puzzle out of each category: **HARDWARE, SOFTWARE, SERVICE PROVIDERS** and **HUMAN RESOURCES**.

- Carry out your learning activities **EVERY DAY**, as often as you can.

- Make sure you focus on **PRONUNCIATION** and **CONVERSATIONS** with other people.

- **MEASURE YOUR PROGRESS** by counting the **REVISION CARDS** learnt.

- Note down your **POSITIVE EXPERIENCES** in your diary.

- Reward your everyday actions with small **PRIZES**.

- Use a **PROGRESS PLOTTER** for monitoring and pacing your progress.

- Combine your language learning with things you're already **PASSIONATE** about.

- Take advantage of positive **PEER PRESSURE** through **GROUPS, ONE-TO-ONE EXCHANGES, TEACHERS, TUTORS, COACHES, MENTORS ACCOUNTABILITY PARTNERS, STUDY BUDDIES, ROLE MODELS, PRAISE DONORS & LINGUISTIC LIAISONS.**

- Set up **POINTERS** to help remind you to carry out your short language learning activities for when you're distracted, tired or stressed.

- Use a **HABIT FARM** to cultivate your own language learning habits.

- Constantly trap new useful language by **WRITING IT DOWN**, **CHUNKING IT** and **REVISING IT**.

- Be **PATIENT**. Don't try to learn too much, too soon.

- Stay **POSITIVE**. You can do it!

Positive Peer Pressure Providers

Thanks to the following people for their help, support and positive Peer Pressure: Gillian, Gary (and Linda, Gemma and Eli), Catrine, Luca, Cormac and all from BCN Pride Toastmasters, Gemma, Jordi and all from the Som-Hi Toastmaster Club, Nicole and all from the Prestigious Speakers TM Club, Jeff, Alba and all at Toastmasters Plus, to Joana, Anna, Olga, Jordi, Albert, Mariajo, Paula, Annie and all at IPA Productions who helped, to Cadence, Brenda, Charlie, Anne, Becky, Isabella for sharing their experiences, to my frequent and not so frequent language exchange partners Àngel, Agnès, Raúl (Laura & Júlia) and Marc, my teacher/tutors Jenni and Cristian, to Andrew and Patricia from Gallery Of Ideas and to Simon and his hamster.

Biography

Productivity trainer, public speaker, life coach, business owner, company director, playwright and now author, Ian Gibbs was born in Sheffield, England where his family was convinced that due to his shy, retiring nature he would never venture far from home.

After doing his degree in Theoretical Physics, Astronomy and Astrophysics at St. Andrews, Scotland and his Postgrad in Education in Cambridge, he decided he'd had enough of the crap weather and went to work in Barcelona for a year - or maybe two - to teach English. One day he woke up to realise he's now been there for 25 years, during which time he has set up one of Europe's leading educational Theatre-in-English companies: IPA Productions, he has written regular life-style columns for two Spanish magazines, was the guest blogger for the local business networking group.

He now coaches the expat community and gives business training sessions on productivity and public speaking. When he is not training, coaching or speaking, he writes. He is the creator of 10 plays for children, 3 comic strips, 3 plays for adults, one bilingual story book, the USSB model for improving personal productivity and numerous personal development articles.

'Learning a Language: How I managed it. How you can, too' is his second book. His first book *'The Sorites Principle: How to harness the power of perseverance* (Guid Publications, 2016) is available both in English and Spanish.

He is married, has two children and a bouncy dog.

The Sorites Principle: How to harness the power of perseverance

Ian Gibbs

Everyone knows the stuff about 'a journey of a thousand miles begins with a single step' but few of us actually make the most of it. This is because it's misleading. The successful journey of a thousand miles begins with a lot of planning and preparation for those difficult times to come. It also involves learning how to cultivate a resilient perseverance that will keep you going when you start to confuse slow progress with no progress.

This book looks at how to apply the Sorites Principle (that the constant application of insignificant actions when coherently focussed will inevitably lead to dramatically significant results) and how to overcome the feelings of futility, procrastination and the inevitable lack of willpower.

Whether you want to lose weight, learn a new language, become a film director, write your first book or just want to keep your home clean and tidy, the Sorites Principle may be just what you need: a powerful unification of tips, tricks and techniques on how to achieve great things via small efforts.

So take your first step towards your life goals by reading this book and start achieving your dreams today.

If you'd like to download and print off some very practical and useful worksheets to help measure your progress, you can find them here:

http://www.guid-publications.com/soritesworksheets/

For more of our books, visit: http://www.guid-publications.com

Printed in Great
Britain
by Amazon